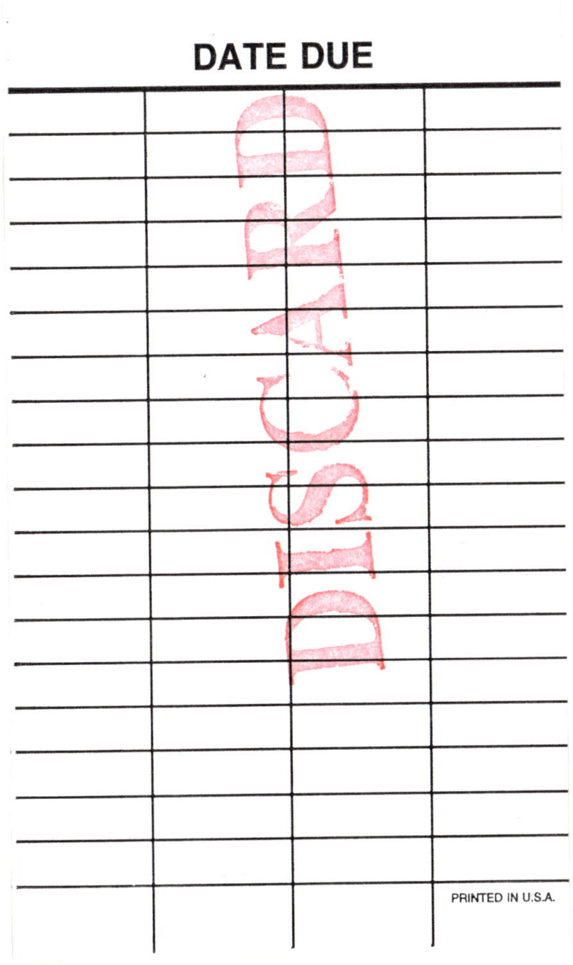
DATE DUE
DISCARD
PRINTED IN U.S.A.

# ORGANIC LITERACY

*The Keywords Approach to Owning Words in Print*

**Kathy R. Fox**

**Chelsey Bahlmann**

**Joy Foster Hughes**

**Melissa Milstead**



**University Press of America,® Inc.**
**Lanham · Boulder · New York · Toronto · Plymouth, UK**

4501 Forbes Boulevard
Suite 200
Lanham, Maryland 20706
UPA Acquisitions Department (301) 459-3366

10 Thornbury Road
Plymouth PL6 7PP
United Kingdom


Printed in the United States of America
British Library Cataloging in Publication Information Available

Library of Congress Control Number: 2012951866
ISBN: 978-0-7618-6047-1 (clothbound : alk. paper)
eISBN: 978-0-7618-6048-8

Cover photos by Kristi Wetherill

™ The paper used in this publication meets the minimum requirements of American National Standard for Information Sciences—Permanence of Paper for Printed Library Materials, ANSI Z39.48-1992

# DEDICATION

To Ramakhetse, Jesse and Ismael, for showing me what works,
& to A.,G., & L., for your patience and support.

*K.R.F.*

To my sister, Whitney, Mom and Dad.

*C.B.*

To my loving husband for always encouraging me to strive for greatness & to my students for your continued inspiration.

*J.F.H.*

To Rocco, my family, and colleagues for your love and support & to my students for the many lessons you have taught me.

*M.M.*

## CONTENTS

## *Preface*

> *Hi Dr. Fox!*
> *I wanted to share with you what happened today...I had a great Keywords experience! I was reading with one of my students this morning during a guided reading lesson. He figured out the word "card" in the book because one of his key words was "car"... Thank you for teaching us about Key Words - I can't wait to start it Day One next year!-Amy. See you in class tomorrow night!*[1]

This excerpt comes from an experienced Kindergarten teacher, who is also enrolled in a graduate literacy program. Her comments compliment the many correspondences and conversations I've had with colleagues and teachers describing their classroom experiences with the organic nature of literacy, when based on a child's own personal bank of words. First inspired by Sylvia Ashton Warner, and then adapted to fit my own classroom, this methodology is based on the essential theory of organic language...the native urge to write and read the spoken word.[2] Through my own practice, I have seen this methodology literally light up the faces of hundreds of children. In discussions regarding literacy with parents, colleagues, and most recently, seeing it implemented in the classrooms of the teachers in my university development community, I have been able to share the success of the methodology with others. *Where can I get more information? Can you visit my school to watch my children do Keywords? I'm so amazed at how easy it is to get started!* And, *why haven't I learned about this earlier!* are common questions I've heard from teachers in the field. However, writing a book on Keywords has come slowly to me, as I have always referred the teacher or parent to Ashton-Warner's own original work on the subject. Her writing continues to inspire me, especially the images of Maori children in her school setting, and the originality of the children's script included in the text. The ongoing interest in her work reinforces the clarity and timelessness of Ashton-Warner's concept of organic language, which I have come to recognize in the broader sense of the term, organic literacy. In spite of the cyclical changes in the politicized nature of public education, it can never be forgotten that *meaning* is central to literacy and that writing—expressive—and reading—interactive—go hand in hand for the very young.

This book reiterates for the reader that there exists an inner world, and along with it, a native urge to express this world in print.[3] Three beginning teachers, modeling their practices on initial work by Sylvia Ashton-Warner, have collaborated with me to write a "how-to" book on adapting and implementing the methodology, called Keywords, for today's classrooms. Additional inspiration and ideas are included from classrooms with specific designations, such as English Language Learners (ELL), adult English as a Second Language (ESL) students, children with special needs and those in an afterschool remedial reading program. Our hope is that the book encourages readers to look for the "organic" nature of writing, to listen to a child's "key vocabulary,"[4] and to value the emotional and physical connection of the spoken to the written word. Trust in a young child's purpose for writing is key and will allow words to emerge!

## NOTES

1. Personal correspondence from Amy Blessing. May 5, 2010.
2.Sylvia Ashton-Warner. *Teacher* (New York: Simon & Schuster, 1963).
3. Ibid, 32.
4. Ibid, 41.

## ACKNOWLEDGEMENTS

We are grateful to the many teachers who have shared their own success stories of using Keywords in their classrooms, most especially Amy B., Amy F. and Sarah. We also want to acknowledge the teachers and researchers who have taught us about Ashton-Warner's work. The resources included in this book, particularly the research of Sydney Gurewitz Clemens and that of Susan Middleton, were important to understanding her historical context.

A special thanks to all the children who have shared their inner worlds with us, making us laugh and sometimes cry with their honesty and clarity about what really matters in life. Thank you to our families for their support, both technical and emotional, in this writing process.

# *Chapter 1*
# An Introduction to Keywords

> *My favorite thing about key-words is having and working on my writing, and I get to share my feelings and choose my own key-word.*[1]

The reoccurring interest in Sylvia Ashton-Warner's work fifty years since the first publishing date of *Teacher,*[2] her most popular book, maintains the clarity and timelessness of Ashton-Warner's conception of early literacy. It reinforces that meaningfulness is central to literacy. It emphasizes that writing and reading are just as connected for the very young as we expect them to be for the mature reader.

Ashton-Warner worked as a primary teacher of children whose home language, culture and literacy background differed from her own and from much of the curriculum she was mandated to teach. Through her classroom experiences she discovered that the five and six year olds did not have the same rudimentary knowledge of print as assumed by the required curriculum. Taking a risk, she began reading and writing practices with the children to discover and build upon what they *did* know. She developed these practices into a literacy methodology that uncovered what natural language *was* important to them. She called this methodology "organic reading."[3]

Ashton-Warner began the day in her classroom by acknowledging each child's organic language. In her classroom every child was given the opportunity to read and write a new word of their choosing, thereby developing a sense of ownership of their printed and spoken vocabulary. In this way a one-to-one correspondence between the spoken word and print was developed. The two concepts—ownership of print through choice of personal text and one-to-one correspondence with spoken and printed word—were in many cases missing from the children's lives outside of the classroom. Ashton-Warner, rather than viewing the lack of school-like literacy in the home as a deficit, operated from what was then a revolutionary idea...that the children's native lifestyles and stories were valid and should be included in classroom discourse.

Ashton-Warner's work has been important to me as a teacher from several different perspectives. It was first introduced to me in my own teacher education program in the late 1970's. At the time I did not yet understand the disconnect between children's organic vocabulary and that produced in their school texts. However, my first few teaching assignments quickly helped clarify the idea that children have something meaningful to say and that their voices are powerful to them. Their spoken words can then become valued texts. Secondly, for minority language children within a majority language school system, recognition of one's home language is the key to expressing one's self. Owning the word opens up the possibility for discourse whereas shutting out one's voice by not acknowledging the child's choice of words can serve to cut off discourse. Thirdly, the success of the organic writing methodology showed me again and again how important choice was for children to create their own texts.[4] When asked "What word do you want to learn to write today?" gave validity to the child as a contributing classroom member. Just as acknowledging a person with a "Hello" and "How are you?" sets the tone of a polite conversation, the question, "What word do you want to learn to write today?" validated the children's literate presence in the room. "This is my new Keyword," and "What's your Keyword today?" were starting points of many conversations between children, parents, other teachers and staff members, as well as with me, an interested conversation partner each day. The children expected the question and were interested to discuss their response both with me and their classmates. In other words, it was significant for them.

## WHAT HAS BEEN LEARNED ASHTON-WARNER'S WORK?

A review of the literature on organic language and the implementation of Ashton-Warner's methodology make clear that the notability of her work has not waned but instead appears in cycles. Jeanette Veatch, a well-known champion of teaching reading without basal readers, said even educators can forget the very fundamentals of how children learn literacy.[5] She saw the lack of recognition of organic language as an omission from pedagogical practices of one of the best ways to reach young readers and writers.

Veatch made the point that key vocabulary is child centered, emerging from the child and their first words. To illustrate her point she quoted Ashton-Warner: "First words must have intense meaning. First words must be already part of the dynamic life. First books must be made of the stuff of the child himself, whatever, and wherever the child".[6]

Using Ashton-Warner's organic language methodology, children build literacy by recognizing their own spoken word in its written form. Clemens used Ashton-Warner's description of the "caption of the mind" as a way to understand organic vocabulary, in that the printed form gives physical manifestation to the spoken word.[7] Neumayer said there is a physiological reaction to a word. If a word is emotionally charged there is a physical reaction. As he so clearly put it, "A lie detector responds to words, not individual sounds.

For instance, when we hear *Once upon a time* we settle in for a very special trip."[8]

Mamchur drew this same connection when she compared the organic connection of words to the left hemispherical, linear thinking that continues to dominate discussions about literacy. This more detached approach forgets the natural pulse of the child and presents reading as the translation of symbols on a page.[9] Thompson calls this the "depersonalization of education," characterizing the scripted-ness of the school day as homogenized learning. Thompson says of Ashton-Warner that she legitimized the role of emotion in education: "Researching into the child's mind through open and personal communication, without judgment, she was able to identify feelings, interests and knowledge upon which to build literacy learning".[10]

Examining instruction across economic levels shows that often the more affluent the school's population the more flexible the curriculum. McQuillan[11] reported that teachers in poor districts were more likely to rely on phonics-based instruction to teach reading. Scripted, direct instruction programs have been shown to limit materials in the classroom. Jaeger, a California teacher, described the impact of Reading First, a program that targeted students at risk of failing at reading through a scripted curriculum, as:

> The district shackled the teachers of poor children with generally lower achievement to a curriculum that did not let them modify their teaching. Teachers in more affluent schools could enrich the curriculum to emphasize higher level thinking and aesthetics.[12]

Outside the school setting, Neuman and Celano[13] found less access to print in low income communities. Thus, children who see less of their own personal print vocabulary in the school setting, will likewise have less opportunities to see their personal vocabulary in print in their communities. As in Ashton-Warner's classroom, the challenge is to have high expectations for an organic connection to literacy through meaningful connections to print. Wasserman described such a school in this way:

> My eyes scan the classroom. Bulletin boards "owned" by the children display poems, stories, artwork, and newspaper clippings with headlines...I am immediately reminded of Sylvia Ashton-Warner's advice to teachers: "Let life come in the door." If these are the headlines that children see on newsstands and on the kitchen tables in their homes, why should they not be put under thoughtful scrutiny in the classroom?...[14]

In this same school, when student data on writing development was reviewed in grades 5, 6, and 7 there was a 40% increase in the number of children meeting or exceeding expectations in literacy. The principal related that the key was the attitude of teachers towards high expectations for all children while at the same time trust in the child-centered curriculum.

> The teachers hold the keys...Teachers must see the school as a place where all children can satisfy their curiosity, develop their abilities and talents, pursue their interests, and, through their interactions with their teachers and the older children around them, get a glimpse of the great variety and richness of life.[15]

This parallel continues to be seen today in the work of teachers described here. The school systems hold teachers accountable to teach literacy according to benchmarks at a given grade level as well as federal and state normed reading and writing scores. The teachers described here however saw a rationale that included the individual child's organic language in developing literacy as a meaningful activity. Like Ashton-Warner they sought ways to include organic language alongside state and federally mandated programs. From Ashton-Warner's own struggles to reconcile the structured, linear curriculum with her children's spontaneous language, we drew a parallel to current issues with a prescribed curriculum and the need to recognize the children's organic language. The need to discover the organic vocabulary of each child rings just as clearly today as it did fifty years ago and substantiates Ashton-Warner's belief that all children have something to say. Sylvia Ashton-Warner urged us to remember that learning must be relevant; it must be able to be used in multiple contexts and from today until tomorrow. Today this may seem obvious, but in the 1950's the traditional approach to teaching and learning saw children as empty vessels to be filled by all-knowing teachers. Children were evaluated on their ability to memorize and repeat information. Today Ashton-Warner's theoretical perspective today would be categorized as constructivism[16], valuing children's learning as constructed with others. In coining the term, "the organic nature of learning,"[17] she described the best way to stoke a child's hunger to read and write as to focus on the events that made up their daily lives. She wrote:

> Back to these first words; to these first books. They must be made out of the stuff of the child itself. I reach a hand into the mind of the child, bring out a handful of the stuff I find there, and use that as our first working material ...and in this dynamic material, within the familiarity and security of it, the Māori finds that words have intense meaning to him, from which cannot help but arise a love of reading.[18]

The timeliness of a Keyword revival is supported by Ashton-Warner's belief that an empowered teacher can empower young readers and writers. In today's teaching climate both new and more experienced teachers can look to her for inspiration. The voices of the teachers included here reach out to invite more teachers to experience the voices of their children by sharing stories of Keywords in their own classrooms. The book continues in Chapter 2 with a bit of history of Ashton-Warner and her classroom in New Zealand, important as it situates her in the timeline of the development of public education in the US. Following, in Chapter 3, I describe implementation of Keywords in my classroom. It then transitions to the stories of current teachers all in their first years of teaching—a kindergarten teacher (Chapter 4), a first grade teacher

(Chapter 5) and a second grade teacher (Chapter 6), with adaptations for each grade level and developing literacy growth. In Chapter 7 I emphasize the importance of Keywords for English Language Learners, both in primary school and as adult students in an English as a Second Language course. Chapter 8 provides examples of adaptations made by other teachers, including a special education teacher, and a teacher working in an after-school remedial reading program. The following chapter, Chapter 9, explores how any teacher can implement a version of organic vocabulary through Keywords in their classroom. The final chapter, Chapter 10, provides concluding evidence from classrooms that language is organic when children are given the opportunity to express themselves through their own meaningful vocabulary choices. Appendices include actual lists of Keywords from our classrooms in order to show the patterns in children's words across grade levels and settings, as well as the power of the words to tell a story.

## NOTES

1. Response from Second Grader, February 13, 2009.

2. Sylvia Ashton-Warner, *Teacher* (New York: Simon & Schuster, 1963).

3. Ibid, 35.

4. Ibid, 51.

5. Jeanette Veatch, "From the Vantage of Retirement," *The Reading Teacher* 49, no. 7 (1996): 510-516.

6. Sylvia Ashton-Warner, *Teacher*, 35.

7. Sydney G. Clemens, *Pay Attention to the Children: Lessons for Teachers and Parents from Sylvia Ashton-Warner* (Napa, California: Rattle OK Publications).

8. Peter Neumeyer, "The Art of the Word: Significance in Stories for Young People," *The English Journal* 66, no. 5 (1977): 28.

9. Carolyn Mamchur, "Heart beat," *Educational Leadership* 40, no. 4 (1983): 14.

10. NancyThompson, "Sylvia Ashton-Warner: Reclaiming Personal Meaning in Literacy Teaching," The *English Journal* 89, no. 3 (2000).

11. Jeff Macquillan, *The Literary Crisis: False Claims, Real Solutions* (Portsmouth, NH: Heinemann 1998).

12. Beth Jaeger, Silencing Teachers in an Era of Scripted Reading," *Rethinking Schools* 20, no. 3. (2006): 40.

13. Susan Neuman and Donna Celano, "Access to Print in Low-Income and Middle-Income Communities: An Ecological Study of Four Neighborhoods," *Reading Research Quarterly*, 36, (2003): 8-26.

14. Selma Wasserman, "Dare to be Different: Can a School Choose its Own Path Despite the Pressures of Accountability?" *Phi Delta Kappa*, 88, no.5 (2007): 384.

15. Ibid, 388.

16. George Hruby, "Sociological, Postmodern, and New Realism Perspectives in Social Constructionism: Implications for Literacy Research," *Reading Research Quarterly* 36, no. 1 (2001): 48-62.

17. Sylvia Ashton-Warner, *Teacher,* 51.

18. Ibid, 35.

## *Chapter 2*
## A Historical Context for Sylvia Ashton-Warner

> *I have a very good time with choosing my own keyword because my teacher gives it to me and I say thank you because I love my teacher very much. I love my key-word also.*[1]

The child discussing her Keyword here was born some sixty years after Sylvia Ashton-Warner's first exploration of what she came to call organic vocabulary. She wrote, "I do not recollect in tranquility".[2] Although she was most likely referring to the trial and error attempts at developing her teaching methodology, one might speculate she would make the same comment regarding her life. Today referred to as a revolutionary educator and leading founder of the whole language movement, her path to notoriety was turbulent. Although not a tranquil memory, she would most likely be proud of her renown as a fearless banner carrier for what are still referred to as the "reading wars".[3]

Sylvia Constance Ashton-Warner was born in 1908 in Stratford, Taranaki, located on the Western side of New Zealand's North Island. She was the fifth of eight children. Her father, Francis Ashton-Warner, was 16 when he arrived in New Zealand from England in 1877. He worked as a laborer across the islands. Sylvia's mother, Margaret Maxwell, was a teacher whose family originated from Scotland. She was a tough woman and a survivor. She was a strict teacher, which often resulted in conflict with the educational authorities. This contributed to the family's tendency to move from place to place. Sylvia attended ten small schools, usually taught by her mother. Sylvia's mother had ambitions for her, however, and drove her to succeed. In handwriting, her mother forced Sylvia to use her right hand against her natural left-handedness, a practice that was common at the time. True to form, Sylvia maintained her left-handedness, leaving her with an unusual ambidexterity. She could write a sentence from both ends and join it neatly in the middle. Sylvia chose to follow in her mother's footsteps, becoming a teacher. She completed the course to qualify for teacher training in Auckland. There she began to express herself and wanted to pursue a career in the arts. Her classmates characterized her as daring and unconventional: she wore make-up, smoked, and wore exotic outfits to social events. They found her magnetic personality charming, and were impressed by her artistic and musical talents. During her teacher training she met Keith Henderson, a fellow student. They became romantically involved and he proposed to Sylvia just before he left to take a permanent teaching role in Taranaki. She accepted but, as she still had to complete her training, it meant her staying behind and having a long-distance relationship. They eventually married in 1932, in the midst of the Depression. Only a few teaching posts were available and economic times were hard. Keith got another teaching post in Taranaki and Sylvia stayed at home. Their daughter, Jasmine, was born in 1935 and Elliot, their son, in 1937. Sylvia and Keith shared a unique arrangement for the time, as he did much of the housework and homemaking, while she pursued artistic and professional activities. Sylvia and Keith found work together in a remote Māori school on the East Coast of the North Island. Sylvia did not find teaching easy or fulfilling. After a day of teaching, amidst her household chores, she prepared her next day's teaching materials, necessary in the remote areas. Because of native school requirements she learned to speak the Maori language. She also struggled to continue her art and writing. In 1939 Sylvia had what at the time was called a nervous breakdown. She was treated by Dr. Donald Allen, who introduced her to the notion of there being two opposite forces at work in the world: survival of the individual and survival of the species. These two forces she would later re-label as Fear and Sex, a concept crucial to the development of her ideas about teaching. Dr. Allen also encouraged Ashton-Warner to write as a form of therapy.

Eventually Sylvia began to find a sanctuary in the primary school classroom. This sanctuary she called 'Selah', a Hebrew word from the Old Testament Psalms which meant, for her, a pause or rest. Having such a space for herself was important for Sylvia's internal well-being. Selah became a tradition she maintained throughout her life, calling it her "creative space".[4]

Sylvia's educational ideas continued to evolve. She found additional sanctuary in the children's language. She encouraged the Māori children to express their own stories in words, music and dance. These new texts related to the children's experiences, rather than the conventional books written from a distant culture and place. She began to write her own 'text books' for the Māori children, using as much of the children's key vocabulary as possible.

Sadly, Ashton-Warner continued to suffer from emotional difficulties, increasingly seeking solace in alcohol. World War II was an additional threat. Family duties now included taking in a sister who had fled the capitol from fear of bombing. She attended War Institute meetings. The violence associated with the war may have influenced her beliefs about the prevalence of fear in the child's inner world: "The violence I believe to be in all of us is subdued in the undermind, waiting, but which blasts out on occasion depending on how near to the surface it is, or on the rigidity of the surface".[5] Rather than subduing the violence, she believed that children needed to release it, "by relating through words the outside of a child to the inside of a child and then you'd get integration".[6] She believed that creativity was the character trait to combat this pervasive nature of violence.

In 1949 the couple moved to Fernhill, Hastings, on the North Island's East Coast. This is where her ideas, both as a teacher and as a novelist, began to bear fruit. In 1957 the family moved to the largest Māori school in the country at Bethlehem, Tauranga, near the top of the North Island. Her teaching, family, artistic and writing practices were each given space, as she described here:

> I have so much to do between school and home that I have to give every minute its value. I must keep my reading and learning of poetry going and mental exercises: Huxley, Russell and such, from the public library, the new book clubs; one book at least has been suitable: *This Hill is Mine*. Also there is the Maori language to continue learning, schoolwork, scheme, workbook and chart preparation. I practice Maori sentences that Mrs. Hira has taught me; over and over again, whenever I am alone, doing dishes and sweeping...still there is a book to be written; every night, dead or dying, after school work and letters, I get in those few lines.[7]

In 1958 she published the novel, *Spinster.*[8] Following the popularity of Sylvia's teaching methodology and fame as a revolutionary in the profession. This novel would eventually be made into a movie, *Two Loves*, starring Shirley MacLaine in 1961.[9]

Ashton-Warner's teaching methods began to gain national recognition in New Zealand. The magazine *National Education* published her work on *The Māori Infant Room – Organic Reading and the Key Vocabulary.*[10] Paradoxically, at the time of her growing fame as an educator, she became further disillusioned with teaching. Employing her writing skills, however, she compiled her classroom photos and notes and wrote her most famous book *Teacher,* published in 1963, to international acclaim. Through the autobiographical text, Ashton-Warner explained how she helped children to learn to read through writing. She began by inviting them to draw pictures and add their own captions. These first words were immensely important in understanding the organic nature of the process of writing and reading. Ashton-Warner opens her first chapter by explaining how one word can be a "book". She explains: "The Egyptian hieroglyphics were one-word sentences. Helen Keller's first word, "water," was a one-word book…in a famine area the teachers wouldn't think of beginning with any words other than "crop," "soil," "hunger," "manure" and the like".[11] Children shared their one word books and drawings with classmates, giving further meaning to the print. They wrote one word, then two sentences, then three, until six-year-olds were writing half a page a day and seven-year-olds a page or more a day. They built up their words into sentences and created books about their experiences. Ashton-Warner explained the impact of this method:

> The drama of these writing could never be captured in a bought book. It could never be achieved in the most faithfully prepared teaching books. No one book could ever hold the variety of subjects that appears collectively in the infant room each morning. Moreover, it is written in the language that they use

> themselves. The books they write are the most dramatic and pathetic and colorful things I've ever seen on page.[12]

Although *Teacher* was well-received internationally, it received only a lukewarm reception in New Zealand. This was somewhat understandable at the time because of the caustic attitude she expressed towards the educational authorities, including the treatment of Maori natives in school and society. The book made visible the harsh life of a teacher and wife in New Zealand, a daring portrayal at the time, prior to the women's liberation movement to come in the following decades.

Keith Henderson died in 1966. This change in life situation prompted Ashton-Warner to leave New Zealand and explore her independence and love of travel, as well as continuing to write. For the remainder of her life she travelled internationally, often to work on educational projects – such as in Israel, America and Canada. In 1971 she took a position at the Simon Fraser University in Vancouver, Canada. She ran twice-weekly sessions, implanting theory through 'The Vancouver Project', which introduced the method into several Vancouver primary schools. In 1972 Sylvia Ashton-Warner published *Spearpoint*[13] about her experiences and work on a pioneering approach in Aspen, Colorado. The book commented on the 'de-sensitization' of American children, which she attributed to watching too much television. Although some thought she was too critical in her reporting, particularly of the work done by teachers in Aspen, the project proved quite successful. She continued in Aspen and worked in the more agreeable role as a 'Teacher of Teacher-Trainers'. She encouraged teachers to help children find their first words in print from those that held significance for them. She set up her living room as a model infant room and took groups of trainees in a 'Key Vocabulary' lesson. She soon had a social network of adoring fans. One devoted group of educators was so influenced by her work that they began to call themselves Sylvians.[14]

Sylvia again became unhappy and returned to New Zealand. With health problems her issues with alcohol returned. However she eventually began working on writing projects, such as cooperating on a television documentary about her work. During this period she wrote her autobiography, *I Passed This Way,* published in 1979.[15] Suffering from the effects of various operations, however, Sylvia grew weaker. Elliot, her son, spent a year helping to care for her. Jasmine and he were by her side when Sylvia died in April 1984. Despite her idiosyncratic behavior—or maybe because of it—Sylvia Ashton-Warner made several key contributions to education. Perhaps the greatest of these contributions was enabling students to develop their personal literacy by drawing on their own experiences. She promoted the beliefs that learning must be real, relevant and rewarding, and applied this to her own life as well.

Ashton-Warner's notion of race, civil rights and social justice must be put in the context of her time. Her teaching methodology was not designed to promote bilingualism or multicultural appreciation. However the context of the time, just following World War II and preceding 1968 civil rights legislation in the US, made the methodology of valuing multiple voices particularly meaningful. She described it as "a bridge from the known to the unknown; from a native culture to a new: and universally speaking, from the inner man out".[16] This pedagogical context made it possible for her to develop her educational theories, studying the Maori child as a symbol of cross cultural flux. In her novel *Greenstone*,[17] the character, Hui, a child of mixed race, crosses back and forth across a river between "This" (her English side) and "That" (her Maori side). Sylvia saw her key vocabulary methodology as a means of valuing children's own words as their beginning texts, as a bridge between cultures, each affecting the other towards maintaining a successful balance. Ideally she longed for this bridge to be two-way, or transcultural, as a two-way bridge between cultures, each affecting the other.[18] Sylvia Ashton-Warner believed people developed best when giving voice to their own experiences. This theme has continued to be pursued by people who want to empower individuals and communities. Sylvia's recognition that each person has a 'key vocabulary'[19], a set of words with a special meaning relating to their emotional life, enabled her to develop a literacy scheme for children who were otherwise failing at school. Such an approach enables children to see meaning in print and is more likely to help them to develop their own literacy and shape their future lives. The Talimi Haq School in Howrah-Calcutta, India, which focuses on sustaining creativity of the economically depressed children it serves, uses Ashton-Warner's approach for helping students maintain Urdu, their native language. This organic approach develops what is already within; rather than imposing from outside. As one entry from the school's blog describes:

> Language education in such [traditional school] environments throws up challenges, since the sought after language (English) is very far away from the children's social environment, and their own language, Urdu, is a second-rate or third-rate option, clearly understood to bring with it a second-rate or third-rate future. At the same time, through building a sound foundation through the mother tongue, Urdu, the felicity in language learning that young children have is something that should be taken advantage of. The possibility of new social and economic avenues and opportunities that the language ability opens up has also to be grasped.[20]

One of the school's blog pages quotes Ashton-Warner as saying:

> *By organic, I mean that way of growth where the strongest thing pushes up ahead of the less strong. I think of trees growing in a clump. The strongest get to the light. In speaking of a child's mind I mean the strongest impulses push up, irrespective of whether or not they should, at any given time...*[21]

Another devotee wrote about her work with her own young children, saying that by using the key vocabulary method, her children learned to read and write "earning respect for and by their families". She said, *"Like Sylvia I can say, 'I know all this because I've done it.'"*[22]

## NOTES

1. Response from Second Grader, February 13, 2009.
2. Sylvia Ashton-Warner. *Teacher* (New York: Simon & Schuster, 1963): 15.
3. Nicholas Lemman, "The Reading Wars" *Atlantic Monthly* 280, no. 5 (1997): 128-134.
4. Sylvia Ashton-Warner. *Myself* (New Zealand: Whitcombe and Tombs, 1967).
5. Sylvia Ashton-Warner. *Teacher* (New York: Simon & Schuster, 1963): 32.
6. Sylvia Ashton-Warner. *Myself,* 110.
7. Ibid, 28.
8. Sylvia Ashton-Warner. *Spinster.* (London: Secker and Warburg, 1958).
9. *Two Loves*, film, directed by Charles Walters (1961, Los Angeles: Metro-Goldwyn-Mayer).
10. National Education Foundation. Maori Infant Room: Organic Reading and the Key Vocabulary (New Zealand: National Education, 1 December 1955): 392–393
11. Sylvia Ashton-Warner. *Teacher*, 27.
12. Ibid, 52.
13. Sylvia Ashton-Warner. *Spearpoint.* (New York: Knopf, 1972).
14. Susan Middleton, "Sylvia's Place: Ashton-Warner as New Zealand Educational Theorist" in The Kiss and the Ghost: Sylvia Ashton-Warner and New Zealand, eds. A. Jones and S. Middleton (Sense Publishers, 2009), 39-49.
15. Sylvia Ashton-Warner. *I Passed This Way* (Wellington: Reed, 1980).
16. Sylvia Ashton-Warner. *Teacher*, 28.
17. Sylvia Ashton-Warner. *Greenstone* (New Zealand: Whitcombe and Tombs, 1966).
18. Sylvia Ashton-Warner. *Teacher*, 37.
19. Ibid, 32.
20. Ibid, 27.
21. Looking from Here. Accessed Dec. 28, 2011, http://talimihaqschool.blogspot.com/Looking from here/November 5_2006
22. Sydney G. Clemens, *Pay Attention to the Children: Lessons for Teachers and Parents from Sylvia Ashton-Warner* (Napa, California: Rattle OK Publications): 10.

## *Chapter 3*
## Developing My Own Keywords Style

> Teacher: *What word do you want to learn to write today?*
> Jesse: *Maribel.*
> Teacher: *That's your sister's name isn't it? What letter will it begin with...m/m/m. You're right. Since it's her name I have to use an upper case M, just like the /J/ in your name. Mar-I-b-b-b...what letter makes that sound? You're right, so I will write b-e-l. Maribel.*

The inclusion of children's families and home-lives in an elementary curriculum seems natural. However, it is often up to the teacher to make the decision to do so, bucking against a scripted curriculum that would have asked Jesse to memorize vocabulary words or to complete a worksheet to test his initial consonant knowledge. Instead, in this excerpt from my Kindergarten-1$^{st}$ grade class, Jesse has chosen his most powerful word of the moment—his sister's name. The word provides me with an authentic context for talking about phonological and letter knowledge. Jesse has a purpose for attending to the task; he can talk about, copy, share and eventually recognize his sister's name.

My teaching career began just after my college graduation as a Peace Corps Volunteer in Lesotho, a small country in southern Africa, where Sesotho, a native Bantu language, is spoken. The primary schools used a scripted curriculum modeled on the British system, with assessments based on vocabulary particular to European culture and environment. By Standard 6 those children who remained in school were those who: a) had parents who could continue to afford the yearly tuition; and b) those whose English had progressed enough to pass a national entrance examination to secondary school (approximately 7$^{th}$ grade in US education systems). This of course meant that most of the children did not go beyond early elementary education and books and print did not play a big role in their lives. Returning to the United States I worked as a Head Start preschool teacher, working with 4 and 5 year olds from predominantly Spanish speaking families. Although our objective was not to teach reading and writing, we designed our curriculum using developmentally appropriate practices for promoting early literacy. We included songs, rhymes, finger plays and stories in both English and Spanish. This included an intentional focus to ensure meaningful connections about culturally relevant topics. As a teacher of 4 & 5year olds I particularly looked for culturally relevant vocabulary that would crossover conceptually in both languages, such as Mamá and Mommy, or a song where baby chicks sang "Peep-peep!", much like the "*pío-pío*" of *pollitos* (chicks). I saw that for many of the children, "bike" was the first English word acquired at school. This word was used to describe the heavy duty tricycles we had on our playground. Since there were only four bikes for the twenty or so children, the word was used to negotiate turns, express a need, and create a bond between children as they played together. Daily this one word had power and significance on the playground for children of both language groups, yet few of our books or songs featured this word. To see the word "bike" in print, I would need to use it in a modeled writing lesson.

My first public school job was as a kindergarten teacher in Oxnard, California, again teaching children whose language and culture was different than that represented in many of the reading texts. Most of my students spoke a mixture of English and Spanish, easily and appropriately code-switching between the two languages. They lived in extended and blended family groups in apartment buildings. Their lifestyles outside the school included large family events with rich language and cultural traditions. I saw many of the girls play very traditional gender roles in the playhouse, singing lullabies to dollies and cooking pretend tortillas. Boys, too, dramatized family events, particularly in the block area, building houses and driving block vehicles down imaginary roads. They included talk about animals different from the urban domesticated pets, as many children visited relatives in Mexico during the winter holiday season. *Chivos* (goats), *toros* (bulls) and *culebras* (snakes) were used in oral stories and play, representing mighty animals, rather than the more exotic zoo animals often used in children's texts.

By this point in my teaching experience I recognized myself as a second language learner. I knew how I tended to go about learning words…I learned the vocabulary and phrases that had meaning for my teaching life, rather than what was presented in foreign language instruction. This brought me to explore Ashton-Warner for the second time, this time through the lens of a teacher.

I re-read Ashton-Warner's book *Teacher*[1] in the summer before my second year of teaching kindergarten. As school began I felt confident enough to carve out a block of time to use for Keywords, as I came to call my organic language time with the children. It did not take long at all for me to see how both the children and I began to value this time. It meant that most of the class was involved in activities either independently or with an instructional assistant or parent volunteer. It gave me a listening time, a space to hold conversations, to model and monitor children's oral, written and decoding skills in a brief but focused one on one setting. The children and I came to look forward to the Keyword time of the day…so much so that in the following twenty-one years, with different grade levels, age groups, and language and cultural mixes I continued to use Keywords with every group and with always the same gusto.

As Clemens[2] reiterated Ashton-Warner's words, the proof is in seeing it for one's self.

I now present Ashton-Warner's work as a teacher educator. I work with graduate students in the area of Language and Literacy. Most of my students are already experienced teachers, some having taught in the era of Sylvia Ashton Warner's notoriety and others with just a few years of teaching before returning to graduate school. Some are disillusioned with the structure of their classroom day which is heavily impacted in an atmosphere of summative testing. Many of my students teach children whose home language and culture are different from their own. For the first time they find themselves in the position of being the minority in their own classrooms. They recognize the bridges that must be made in order to lead their students to academic competency while at the same time maintaining cultural pride. I have been pleasantly surprised at how many have embraced Ashton-Warner's work as one way to do this.

## How Did it Work in the Past? How Can it Work Today?

As a public school teacher, I used this methodology, which I have modeled from Ashton-Warner and call Keywords, for more than twenty years. As a teacher educator, I have introduced Keywords to more than two hundred education students who practice their profession in rural to urban areas, low to middle to high income neighborhoods, and with children with varied language needs. With so many qualified teachers using the methodology, several good adaptations and innovations have occurred using Ashton-Warner's methodology as a jumping off place. I begin by describing my own methodology and how it compared with that reported by Ashton-Warner in 1963.

### The Practice in my Classroom

In my own practice I set up my Keywords program much as Ashton-Warner did. Each afternoon before closing my classroom door for the day I like to set up my Keyword table. In that way I could make sure that no matter whatever else interrupted my morning prep time I had Keywords ready to go when the children arrived. I devoted approximately twenty minutes of my morning to the Keyword table. As not all children were able to get their word of the day during that time, I often opened the table up in the afternoon during Center Time as well. On the table I had ready markers, lined 3 x 5 index cards, blank sentence strips and a stapler. The table sat in close proximity to the Keyword chart…a pocket chart with a library-card size pocket for each child's name. As the children entered the classroom, putting away their backpacks, sweaters, lunch boxes, etc., I asked them by name if they wanted a Keyword that day. The table quickly filled. As one child finished another sat down. Within the first twenty minutes of the morning, eight to ten children would have a new Keyword.

The Keyword question I consistently asked my 4, 5, 6 and 7 year old children was "What word do you want to learn to write today?" Just as in Ashton-Warner's classroom, for kindergarteners and 1st graders these words represented everything that was right and/or wrong within their early childhood schema of life. Ashton-Warner divided the organic vocabulary of the children into two categories…creative and destructive. From the giving, intimate or "creative" side of human nature, Ashton-Warner described trends in children's choices of Keywords. Words such as *love*, *heart*, *mom*, *dad* and other words associated with emotional bonds were often chosen.[3] In my own classrooms, over the span of twenty-plus years, the most often repeated words were "love" and "mom", (or variations of this term). Other commonly requested words were names of siblings and color words, especially pink and yellow, often seen as symbolic of love and affection. At the mid-point of each year it seemed a group of children would begin requesting favorite television characters, which would begin a trend until these characters were "used up." These characters were often the names of super-heroes or main characters on children's programming. I valued these words by putting them in print. This is not a time to judge if it is a *good* word, an *age appropriate* word or the *best* word. Instead, it is a time to find out what the child wants to learn…what is important to this child on this day. (For a representative list of Keywords from today's classroom see Appendix A.)

As Ashton-Warner pointed out, sometimes words are difficult to hear from the child, due to the negative or destructive meaning associated with the word. Examples of destructive words I've heard over the years have been *blood*, *knife* and *kill*. Ashton-Warner's work described this same choice of words from her students, decades prior and on a different continent from my experience. In my classrooms I had children who were victims of abuse, children who witnessed abuse of their parents, and children who experienced trauma, such as the loss of a parent, sibling or other significant person. These feelings come out in Keywords. Because my students experienced safety in my classroom it was likewise a safe place to discuss destructive emotions and occurrences.

The choice of words can be seen as an entry way into the child's feelings and culture…what she is bringing into the classroom each day. Likewise, the bonds associated with these words can be capitalized upon to connect meaning to the printed word, which otherwise can seem very abstract to a very young child. In the example given in the opening of this chapter an intimate word, the child's sister's name, was used to attach meaning to the sound symbols in the printed word.

After answering the question, "What word do you want to learn to write today?" I modeled the child's new word by writing it on the index card with a marker. As I spelled out the word I sometimes gave phonetic cues, such as in this example introduced earlier in the chapter. Jesse, a kindergartener, requested his first grade sister's name as his Keyword:

> Tracking my finger under the word, I again read *Maribel.* I now asked Jesse to read the word again before passing it to him.
> Jesse: *Maribel.*
> Jesse then took a sentence strip and began to copy the new word from left to right as many times as would fit on the sentence strip, approximately 3 to 5 times for most words and most young writers.

Ashton-Warner's technique varied in that her students wrote the words on large cards and sometimes on chalkboards.[4] The sentence strips proved to be an effective variation for my students. Many children, especially at the beginning of the year, enjoyed making the strip into what we came to call a Keyword Hat or Crown. As the child finished writing the word, filling the sentence strip with print, I took the strip and made it into a hat, or headband, by stapling it to fit the child's head. As the child left the Keyword table everyone in the room could see and sometimes read the new word. Children asked each other, "What is your word?" and "Can you read my word?"

Often children wore their hats for the greater part of the day. When an adult entered the room inevitably the question came, "What was your word today?" Likewise, if the child wore his/her Keyword hat to the playground, to the office on an errand, or to the cafeteria, other readers were interested in the word of the day. In this way, many opportunities to read their word for the day happened over the course of the day.

Another significant way in which the Keyword was read was when the hat went home with the child that day. At Back-to-School Night and in a teacher-parent letter early each year I explained the Keywords practice so parents understood the significance of the hat. Parents often shared stories with me of their children discussing what their Keyword would be that day or retelling what their classmates' Keywords were on a given day. In this way the Keyword had communicated to parents what their child had viewed as significant to share with me and the other children in the room. This often brought smiles to the parents' faces, as more than once I heard about a new baby or another family even through Keywords.

## How About Today's Teachers and Keywords?

I have found few teachers who would disagree with the idea of organic language, that all children have something to say. Likewise the rationale for Keywords is easily understood...that it reinforces an interest in text to see one's own words in print. However a conceptualization of how this practice can apply across grade level and language backgrounds is more difficult to integrate and the idea of offering this activity on a daily basis may seem almost impossible to visualize. I introduce here three teachers, grades Kindergarten, 1$^{st}$, and 2$^{nd}$, who currently use Keywords methodology in their classrooms. The three teachers were first introduced to the methodology in a graduate level reading class and initially implemented it as an assignment. It was been their choice to continue using Keyword methodology far beyond their assigned practice, and were still using it after graduating from the program. In subsequent chapters additional teachers' work is described, showing that Keywords can be adapted for specific circumstances, such as working with young English language learners, adult second language learners, children with language and speech disabilities, and upper elementary age children who are identified as struggling readers. Children in the schools described here were from diverse socio-economic status and ability levels. The children's home culture and language backgrounds included African American, first generation Latino, Arab American, Mexican American and Anglo American.

## NOTES

1. Sylvia Ashton-Warner. *Teacher* (New York: Simon & Schuster, 1963): 15.
2. Sydney G. Clemens, *Pay Attention to the Children: Lessons for Teachers and Parents from Sylvia Ashton-Warner* (Napa, California: Rattle OK Publications): 10.
3. Sylvia Ashton-Warner. *Teacher*, 44.
4. Ibid, 46-51.

## *Chapter 4*
## Keywords in a Kindergarten Classroom

*Teacher, sitting at a round table with 3 other children busily writing on sentence strips*: Good morning Veronica! How are you doing this morning?

*Veronica, pulling out a chair to sit, index cards in hand*: Good.

*Teacher*: Good. I'm glad to see you at school today! Would you please read me your words?

*Veronica*: Mom, cat, flower, love, horse

*Teacher*: Very good. What word would you like to learn today?

*Veronica* (no hesitation): Play-dough.

*Teacher*: Oooh, play-dough is a lot of fun. What made you think of the word play-dough?

*Veronica*: It is so much fun. Next time I want to learn the word paint. I have a paint set.

*Teacher*: That's great! I know you are very picture smart and make great drawings. Did you know some artists use clay? It is a lot like play-dough in many ways. Ok, let's see if we can work together to write your word. P-p-p-lay-dough... What sound do you hear first?

*Veronica*: P!

*Teacher*: Very good, we hear the /p/ sound which we know is the letter /P/. Watch me write the letter P. I'm going to start on the dotted line since I know this is going to be a lowercase /P/. Then I'll pull straight down into the ground, make a circle, and there's my letter /P/. What do we hear next?

As a first year teacher, I was not completely aware of the challenges I would face teaching a classroom full of diverse learners with varying and vast individual needs. Our school was designated as Title One, a status given to schools where more than half of the children are at a lower economic status. I was not sure what that meant for me as a teacher and how I would adapt what I had learned in my teacher education program and from my new teacher editions of reading and math curriculum to this setting. However, Keywords gave me a solid start.

I was first introduced to Keywords during my final year in an undergraduate education course. My professor explained its origin from Key Vocabulary, a term coined by Sylvia Ashton-Warner. This teaching tool utilizes student-generated words, words that are intrinsically meaningful and special to the child, as a foundation for reading and writing instruction. It allows the child to see the word expressed in written fashion, and provides an opportunity for the child to have a conversation with the teacher regarding why this word is special to him or her. For the teacher, it provides a unique lens into the child's own life. After attending a workshop to see Keywords in action, I decided to implement the program in my own classroom. Without initially being aware of it, I was covering a large portion of the reading curriculum including print concepts, handwriting, phonics and phonemic awareness, as well as vocabulary development. At the time. however, I would have simply stated that I was teaching children to write words which were special to them while simultaneously giving me a chance to get to know the children and build a personal relationship with them. I can now ascertain that without a doubt Keywords is an effective and meaningful tool for teaching the core components of reading; it allows the teacher to use student-generated material, words which are both meaningful and organic to the child, to teach print concepts and vocabulary.

In my second year of teaching, I was given a Kindergarten assignment to teach at the same school. I was not sure how Keywords could be adapted to fit this new range of ages and developmental needs. I decided to implement this methodology in a very similar fashion as Ashton-Warner had done with her youngest children, while keeping in mind the objectives that I would be teaching. At the beginning of Kindergarten, the curricular focus for reading is on concepts of print and reading behaviors. Just as Ashton-Warner's children were most often entering school for the first time, many of my children were coming to me without having attended pre-school or any formal education experiences outside of their homes. Many of them had very little experience with print. Then again, there was the small group who had parents in the home who ensured they entered Kindergarten with multiple experiences with print, in both published books and writing and drawing activities. Some had attended preschool. Keywords quickly became a way for me to get to know my children's needs and levels, and subsequently differentiate my teaching as I worked individually with them at the Keyword table. In my Kindergarten classroom. Keywords became a regular but optional activity. It allowed for student choice, built confidence, and was an effective component of a balanced reading curriculum.

# How does Keywords Methodology Work in a Kindergarten Classroom?

Before the daily routine can be established, I must first introduce Keywords to my class. I quickly learned as a Kindergarten teacher that it is nearly impossible to give detailed instructions to the class as a whole group without having to later repeat them individually. For this reason, I typically introduced Keywords for the first time in a small group of three to four children. I began by explaining to the group that this is a time for them to learn any word which is special to them. I told them it could be a person, thing, place, or simply a word they would like to know how to write. I showed them the key ring on which they will keep their Keywords and tell them multiple times that their Keywords must stay at school, even though a handful of children will repeatedly ask to take their Keyword ring home. I showed them how they will make a "crown" using their new word and that, unlike their key ring of Keywords; they may take their crown home each day. After this simple introduction is done, we begin the daily routine which my class has come to call "learning a word".

Once the routine has been established, Keywords operates the same every day. I typically set up my Keywords table first thing in the morning. I kept a small basket supplied with multi-colored notecards, a marker, a few pencils, a hole puncher, a stapler, and a stack of sentence strips (multi-colored if possible). As the children entered the room they have the option of beginning their morning work or coming to the Keywords table to "learn a word". As the child sat down and we greeted each other, I asked the child to read his/her words to me. I then asked the question: "What word would you like to learn today?" Sometimes the child blurted out the word as soon as he reached the seat, even before I was able to ask my question. If this was the case I repeated, "So you would like to learn the word _____ today?" and continue with the daily routine. The importance of this question cannot be understated as it helped to articulate the idea of "word" for the child, and that the word is the child's choice for what to learn.

After the child told me her word, I often asked something along the lines of, "What made you think of this word?" or "Why is this word special to you?" to help initiate a conversation. This opportunity for conversation between teacher and student was not only a great opportunity for oral language development, but also provided insight into the child's life. As in Sylvia Ashton Warner's classroom, I began to see a pattern in my children's Keyword choices. At the beginning of the year, some children immediately wanted to begin learning the names of their friends, classmates, and pets. "Mom" and "dad" were also popular picks, as is my name and the names of their other teachers. Other children chose words from their sight word list or words they heard and saw frequently in their leveled readers. These included words like "see", "like" and "to". Throughout the year, they were influenced by the thematic units and often wanted to learn related vocabulary. In fall, they often chose words such as candy corn, scarecrow, pumpkin, and spider. Around the winter holidays they oftentimes chose words such as Hanukkah, gift, reindeer, Rudolph, Christmas tree, and star. I was especially excited when they chose to learn the name of an author from a classroom author study, as I saw it as indicative of a personal connection they've made with him or her. Jan Brett, Kevin Henkes and Chris Van-Allsburg have all been Keywords in my classroom.

I enjoyed learning about my children' interests through Keywords, and have learned a lot about pop culture based on the words they chose. For a while "Chihuahua" was a popular Keyword in my class. It seems every child owned (or would like to think they owned) a Chihuahua. It was as a result of this word that I was made aware of the popular children's movie *Beverly Hills Chihuahua*[1], which many of them had seen at the theatre or owned. I could then make a connection to one of our favorite book characters: Skippyjonjones[2], Through this connection I also learned about Jimmy's (pseudonym) cousin who lives with his grandma and has a real Chihuahua named Mario. (For a list of sample Keywords from my classroom, please see the Appendix A: Sample Kindergarten Keywords.)

For the last few years I have also had many children, particularly boys, want to learn the words Transformers, Optimus Prime, and Bumblebee. One of my favorite experiences was with a young kindergartener who had requested the words Optimus Prime, a fictional character from the Transformer™ series. He repeated the word ending several times saying "miss, miss, miss…" before he finally blurted out, "Miss Milstead! That's like your name! Optimus--Miss Milstead! He's the boss like you." I went home that day bragging that I was compared to Optimus Prime by a six year old. Another day I was surprised when a child chose the word "octagon" as her very first Keyword! The information regarding a child's interests that can gained from a simple conversation with a child about his Keyword has continued to amaze and inform me. In addition to the benefits to reading and writing, Keywords has been the catalyst for a mini math lessons and conversations about other academic areas.

After the child has told me his Keyword, I then take a notecard from my basket and have him or her help me spell the word. The child's involvement in this process is dependent on the time of year and the child's literacy level; however, I always articulate what I am doing and why. I sound out the word, emphasizing each letter sound as I write it. I describe the formation of the letters as well. This provides an opportunity to discuss letter sounds, introduce blends and digraphs, practice "stretching" words to hear the individual sounds within it, and see/hear how to form the letters that comprise the word. On occasion a child has asked to learn a word which he was already able to spell, but nevertheless wanted to see it written on paper and included with his special words.

After writing the word, I had the card to the child and have him/her read it back to me. At the beginning of Kindergarten I like to use this opportunity to develop concepts of print. Depending on the child's literacy level and what I am introducing in class, I may have the child point to the first and last letter of the word, count the letters, say each individual letter, or tell me how many words he has on his key ring. After adding the word to the key ring, the child then chose a favorite color sentence strip upon which I wrote the word using a marker, demonstrating once again how to form the letters and the use of appropriate spacing. This modeling of handwriting was especially important for the kindergarten child, as I could adapt it to the individual child's need. At the beginning of the year I usually wrote the word twice and then had the child write the word for the length of the sentence strip. Depending on the child's ability, I may write the word once in a yellow highlighter and have him trace over my printing on the sentence strip. I started at the left side of the sentence strip, modeling the left to right progression of print in English. As the year progressed, I wrote the word once and watched as the child mimicked my writing. The child then wrote the word as many times as could fit across the sentence strip, with me checking for formation of letters and spacing as needed. Finally I measured the child's head with the sentence strip, stapled it to make a crown, and asked him one last time to tell me the word he learned today. Throughout the day other children and teachers will question the child about the word on the crown he is wearing. This served as both a reinforcement of the new word as well as another opportunity for conversation and oral language development.

I next placed the new Keyword on the child's ring, and the child returned to his seat. He then stored his words in his pencil box which he kept in his chair pocket--a fabric pocket that fits across the back of the child's chair. In this way his Keyword collection is easily accessible if he would like to find a word.

Although Keywords is typically a morning activity, I did not rely solely on this block of time. There always seemed to be the handful of children who arrived at school just as the bell rang. They almost always missed the window of time for Keywords. Therefore, I also tried to open the Keywords table at other times of the day when possible. As the year progressed and children grew more independent, I was able to call a few children over to my Keywords table during their independent writing time. Other times I used Keywords as an element of my reading groups. Because Keywords was quick and easy to implement, I could almost always find a time to fit in one or two children's Keywords during different times of the day. I didn't want to miss an opportunity to have this print and oral language activity with as many children as possible. I found myself looking forward to this time with my children as much as, if not more than, they do.

## WHAT IS THE RATIONALE FOR DOING KEYWORDS WITH KINDERGARTENERS DAILY?

As a teacher I am so excited by the power of Keywords. I have seen young children who cannot identify a single letter of the alphabet read their list of fifteen words to me perfectly because Keywords made such a powerful connection from their lives to print. Keywords expanded vocabulary, helped children develop concepts of print, improve handwriting skills, teach spelling patterns, and fostered oral development. The simple act of sharing one's words with another child, hearing the teacher ask on a daily basis, "Read me your words" and asking others, "How many words do you have?", helped children conceptualize the idea of a "word". Naming the letters as we wrote the word, going over the formation of the letters, and talking about the spelling patterns across words, helped the child understand that letters have sounds and can be put together to form words. For a child who has had minimal experience with texts, these are valuable lessons; using meaningful material, in this case the child's own unique organic vocabulary, made these lessons all the more effective.

Aside from the obvious instructional benefits there are social benefits to Keywords. As a result of this program, not only is the teacher able to build a personal relationship with the child and talk with children individually each day, but Keywords also helps foster collaboration and cooperation among my children. During writing time, children instinctively pull their Keywords out from their pencil boxes and have them on the table in front of them. If a child is struggling to spell a word, and another child has that word on his ring, it is not unusual to see that child carry his words over to the child in need. Just as between the teacher and the child at the Keyword table, Keywords sparked conversation between children. It was always wonderful to hear a child point to another child's words and say "I have that word too!" Children discover quickly if they have similar likes and interests with other children based solely on their Keywords.

Keywords are meaningful to children. They are part of what Ashton-Warner referred to as their organic vocabulary[3] and therefore an integral part of who these children were, not just as children within a class but also as individual in a learning community. Keywords allow the teacher to tap into who the child is as a literate being. It provides an opportunity for meaningful vocabulary acquisition, builds confidence, and fosters motivation. Even the least engaged children are drawn into literacy through Keywords. The fact that a struggling reader may not have known the letters of the alphabet or have mastered print concepts but yet could name and identify every Keyword attest to the validity of this teaching tool in my classroom.

The natural reward that comes with success makes Keywords a motivating practice. In this sense, Keywords has been a valuable tool with struggling writers as well. This set of words derived from the child's organic vocabulary, is made easily accessible throughout the day. They may use their Keywords during morning work, writers' workshop, shared reading, or anytime during the day they needed a language resource. As a result, children have come to my table to read their words and I could see that they had written the word multiple times, colored the notecard, drawn a picture to match it, or written other words on the back of the card. It was important to keep their Keywords easily accessible so that children could design their own use for their words, which often included the transfer to other aspects in their writing. This demonstrated to the child that they were each writers with a unique message to share with their readers. As teachers, we want our children to have a love of literacy. Why not capitalize on something they already love? It was not unusual for my children to name Keywords as their favorite time of the instructional day. Keywords reach each and every one of my children by valuing them as individuals. I have found it to be an indispensable way for me to get to know my children and build a personal relationship with them.

## NOTES

1. *Beverly Hills Chihuahua*, film, directed by Raja Gosnell (2008, Los Angeles: Walt Disney Pictures).
2. Judy Schacher, *Skippyjon Jones* (New York: Dutton, 2003).
3. Sylvia Ashton-Warner, *Teacher* (New York: Simon & Schuster, 1963).

# *Chapter 5*
# Keywords in a First Grade Classroom

> The children have their book-bags on and are lined up at the door for dismissal. Children have taken their Keywords out of their pockets to take home, as it is the last day of the quarter. The classroom is loud with an excited buzz and the usual end of the day chatter.
>
> Teacher: Maria, what do you do with your Keywords at home?
>
> Maria: I use them to teach my mom English.
>
> Teacher: Really!? That is great Maria! You're her teacher!

This casual conversation caused me to reflect on Maria's word choice in the past few weeks. Had her word choice been influenced by what she perceived mother wanted—or needed—to learn? Were there other uses for Keywords that I hadn't imagined?

## WHAT DOES KEYWORDS LOOK LIKE IN A 1ST GRADE CLASSROOM?

In my first grade classroom there were typically anywhere between 20 to 25 children. In a typical year about half of the children were white, English speaking and the other half were Latino, with varying levels of English fluency. Five of the children were classified by state and school designation as English Language Learners. The school was located in a low-income area where families worked blue collar jobs; many families struggled to put food on the table and clothing on children's backs. The majority of the families put education as a high priority and wanted their children to graduate from high school and go beyond, perhaps to the nearby university. The school was designated as a Title I school, meaning at least 50 percent of the children in the school were from low-income families. Phonics instruction was the adopted curricular focus for reading at the school. Direct Instruction reading programs were the enforced initiatives at the school. Being a first year teacher, I felt comfortable with these programs. They were easily laid out and I did not have to search for my own resources. I was confident in the system because it was a researched based program with proven results, and because of this I hoped that the program would teach children to read. However, by the end of year 2 of using the program I felt there was something missing. While the Direct Instruction phonics program offered children time for inquiry I felt that, as a teacher, my personal creativity was left out and that the children' interests were overlooked due to the programs rigid structure. Halfway through my first year of teaching I decided to go back to school for a Master's degree in Language and Literacy. I chose this program in pursuit of finding the personalization and child centered approach to literacy that I was searching for.

Lo and behold, I was introduced to Keywords during my first summer course and was intrigued immediately. My professor at the time explained how she used Sylvia Ashton-Warner's Keywords in her first grade classroom. I became interested right away because it was a technique for teaching children to read that allowed children to hold the reigns in what I visualized as the children driving their own learning. This is exactly what I had been hoping to find to break away from the confines of a scripted reading program. Sylvia Ashton-Warner's words inspired me: "What a dangerous activity reading is: teaching is. All this plastering on of foreign stuff. Why plaster on at all when there's so much inside already? So much locked in? If only I could get it out and it as a working material".[1] I was excited to begin Keywords with my first graders, and I was anxious to find out for myself if what I had heard about Keywords and read in Ashton-Warner's *Teacher* would be valid in my classroom. I really wanted to find out for myself if allowing children to 'own' their words would make an impact on their literacy.

When thinking about the implementation of Keywords in my classroom I first had to decide how to fit Keywords into my daily schedule. I knew that the school mandated Direct Instruction program was very demanding and left little room for any additions or adaptations. In order to gain my principal's support I would need to implement Keywords as an addition to the existing program. Ashton-Warner suggested to" take the Key Vocabulary in the morning output period when the energy is the highest, since it is a creative activity, and I believe that the creative activities are more important than anything else...I want to catch the first freshness."[2] I decided Keywords would be the first activity as the children walked in the door to my classroom. As children entered the classroom, a folder of their morning work was at their desks. I sat at the round Keywords table greeting each child as they entered, ready to hear Keywords. Beside the table I had a poster board with library pockets attached, one pocket for each child. Each library pocket was labeled with a child's name, and was where each child kept his or her Keywords. On the center of the Keywords table was a basket with index cards, markers, crayons, a stapler, blank sentence strips, and a dictionary. Children had the choice if they wanted to come over for Keywords each day. This was important because I did not want children to feel this activity was forced on them. I wanted it to be enjoyable and I wanted to make sure their Keywords were sincerely 'organic'[3] words. I have never had a child who refused to come to the Keywords table. Each child was eager to come to the table and share this moment with their teacher. As children approached the table I pulled out an index card and asked "What word would you like to learn today?" The child said his or her word. Prior to writing the word on the index card I incorporated the phonics instruction that children were learning with the Imagine It!™ Reading Program.[4] I said the word slowly and asked if they knew what letters the word contained. I then wrote the word on the index card. Occasionally, I would need to look up the spelling of some of the children's words in the dictionary or on the computer. I believe this modeling of the use of reference resources was a learning experience along with the Keywords because it showed children how to use resources if they needed to find the spelling of a word. Once the word was written I asked children *why* they chose their word. This inquiry provided a peek into each child's world when discussing their responses. I was able to gauge the child's mood, interests, and feelings when they responded. The child would take the index card with their Keyword and a blank sentence strip and write their Keyword as many times as would fit on the sentence strip. Occasionally children would draw a picture to go along with their Keyword, but most would write the word. I then stapled the sentence strip around the child's head to wear the remainder of the day.

Before putting their Keywords into their pocket they would review all of their Keywords from the earlier days. If children got stuck on a word and could not remember what it said I took Ashton-Warner's advice and "destroyed the word because it has failed as a one-look word and couldn't have been much importance to her. And it is the words that are important to her that I am after".[5] The first time a child could not remember a word, I was hesitant to rip up their word and throw it away. I was not sure if there was any emotional attachment to their word, but I decided there was only one way to figure it out. So, I asked the child who was having trouble remembering his word if it was okay if we got rid of this word and he responded "Yes." I could see the sense of relief on the child's face immediately that he did not have to struggle to remember that word any more.

## How and why does Keywords work?

You may ask, "I see how Keywords works in the classroom, but what is the rationale behind each step?" At the beginning of the day when children were asked what word they would like to learn, the underlying premise here was that children were 'owning' their word. This was one of the few times during the day when children had a say in what they wanted to learn. Keywords is all about what the child wants, and because they 'own' their word they will remember it and be proud to claim the word as 'theirs.' The teacher's next question, "Why did you choose this word?" set up an opportunity for the teacher to peek inside the inner world of the child; I discovered what they were feeling, thinking, and/or worrying about. For example, I had a child who one day chose the word 'cast' as her Keyword for the day. When I asked why she chose this word she got very upset and said that her younger brother had broken his arm over the weekend and was wearing a cast to daycare for the first time. I could tell by how emotional she was in her response that she was very concerned about her brother, and because of Keywords she was able to let me know what was overtaking her thoughts that day. Other children at the table who were listening to our conversation were able to comment about people they knew who were wearing a cast, and it made her feel more at ease. I was able to participate in the discussion but did not need to facilitate it any further, as the other children helped put her at ease. This conversation would likely not have happened without Keywords. There were several instances like the one with the Keyword 'cast' which allowed children to let me to see into their world.

What is the importance of having children wear their words on a hat all day? I have found that first graders, at around six years of age, have an egocentric mindset and they like 'showing off' anything they are good at or proud of. By wearing the Keyword hat around their head all day it allows them a way to 'show off' their word to everyone they came in contact with during the school day. Their friends see their Keyword and are interested in an explanation. Other teachers the child comes in contact with during the day may be curious and spark up a conversation with the child about the Keyword. In this way not only are children hearing others say their word all day, these conversation are help them make additional associations with their conversation partners about the word.

In my classroom I noticed an increase in my child's literacy as a result of using Keywords. For one, my children accumulated several words over the course of a year and these Keywords were reviewed with the children each day. This gave children an opportunity to see and say the words multiple times. I have no doubt that when children were to see these words appear in a text they would be able to identify them. The unfortunate thing is, of course, these Keywords rarely appeared in published texts written for children. I also encouraged children to use Keywords when writing. Children had the opportunity to use their Keywords as they wrote as a spelling reference or to spark ideas for writing. Sometimes children would use each other's Keywords. For example, one of my children, Luis, was writing a story with a Chihuahua in it. Although he did not know how to spell 'Chihuahua' on his own, and did not have it in his own Keyword collection, he knew someone in the class that did. He asked that child for permission to borrow her Keyword. It was interesting how children remembered each other's Keywords as well as their own.

There were a few lessons that I learned through trouble shooting during my first year using Keywords as part of my literacy instruction. One issue I faced was that children accumulated so many words it was hard to store them. I decided at the half way point in the year that children would take their words home each quarter. They were delighted to do so and looked forward to this special day. I wondered, however, what happened to these words once they were sent home. Even though I sent a note home with the words, explaining to the parents that the cards were their child's Keywords for the quarter and it would be beneficial to review these words at home. In my classroom I knew that my children' families were busy and I did not have much confidence that families would really review the words, but it was a 'hope' of mine. One day I was having a conversation with one of my English Language Learners and I asked if she was reviewing her Keywords at home. She responded by saying that she used them at home to teach her mother English. I was taken aback when I heard this comment. I realized that her Keywords were much more than just random words to her; they were words that she wanted to learn, but also words that she would use to teach her mother. I have since wondered if her Keyword choice was influenced by a word that her mother wanted to learn.

While using Keywords with children, gender differences in their word choice emerged. In *Teacher*, Ashton-Warner said "All boys want words of locomotion, aeroplane, tractor, jet, and the girls the words of domesticity, house, Mummy, doll"[6], but that was 1963. However, in my classroom I noticed similar findings. I chose a random sample of females' Keywords and found sparkle, pink, flower, baby, cat, and scarf. A random sample of males' words included stick shift, big truck, and monster truck. Children's Keywords do seem to be influenced by gender, among other factors. (For a list of sample Keywords from my classroom, please see the Appendix B: Sample 1st Grade Keywords.)

In looking at the word lists again, after four years, I can remember a mental image of a child and our conversations about each one of his or her words. This is due to the authenticity of the conversation, sparked by the child's Keyword choice. Ashton-Warner says that children have an inner and an outer eye. The inner is vocabulary chosen by the children and the outer is vocabulary chosen by adults, both can be meaningful, but "it is the captions of the mind pictures that have the power and the light".[7] In order for vocabulary to be meaningful it needs to be authentic, just what the Keywords methodology aims to do. She reinforces the point by adding "...if you were a child, which vocabulary would you prefer? Your own or the one [presented]?"[8]

As a teacher, when you begin something new, it is necessary to go through every scenario in your mind and plan how you will handle it. When planning for the possible scenarios when doing Keywords with first graders, one scenario that I worried about was, what if a child repeats words or wants the same words as their friends? I was prepared if happened and decided that if the child repeatedly wanted the same word as a friend I would tell the child to think of another word. In this way I would emphasize to the child that this was *his or her* word and it would be different than anyone else's in the room. I also decided that if a child wanted to repeat a word again I would allow it in hopes that they would see the consistency of the word and would really be able to read this word. Neither of these scenarios ever played out in my classroom. The children naturally picked up on the fact that the words belonged to them and they never wanted the same words as their friends. They were, however, able to keep up with each other's words, which was demonstrated when they wanted to "borrow" a friend's word during writing time. They were able to remember each other's words and ask the person who had that specific word to borrow their word as a reference.

One thing I had not anticipated was the social networking factor during Keywords. My class would get on theme 'kicks' throughout the year. Often at the beginning of the year they wanted their classmates' names and teachers' names. During the fall they wanted candy corn, monster, and pumpkin, and around the winter holidays they wanted words associated with the season, such as candle, gift, brand names of toys, Santa Claus, and present.

## THE RESEARCH CONNECTION

The importance of knowing the research behind a technique or methodology before implementing in a classroom cannot be understated when working with impressionable first graders. I knew from my own action research that Keywords was having a positive impact on my children' reading and writing. Children were able to read their own Key vocabulary and transfer this knowledge into the books they were reading and they were able to spell these words correctly in their own writing. I wanted to know how other research compared. A study that looked at kindergarten and first grade children in four different cities supplied further evidence of the effects of Keywords.[9] The researchers examined the following questions:

1. Is there a significant difference in the words children are asked to learn in the Sylvia Ashton-Warner approach and the words presented in pre-primers and primers of basal reading series used in their school systems?
2. Is there a difference in the words requested by children in four cities in different geographic areas of the United States?
3. Is there a difference in the basic vocabulary presented in the pre-primers and primers for basal reading series?[10]

The findings indicated that in three out of the four schools the Keywords had little to no relationship with the words presented in the basal readers. The words found in the basal series had little correlation to the Keywords that the children chose. All four schools found similar Keyword choices among the participating children. The research indicated that:

> It seems reasonable, therefore, that the children's own key vocabulary is more meaningful than the basal reader vocabulary. Thus, it may be easier for some children to use their own Keywords elicited by the Sylvia Ashton-Warner approach in learning to read, spell, and express their thoughts in writing[11]

As a teacher in my sixth year of teaching and who has already seen and used several methods for literacy instruction, I know that there is not one true method that works for all children. However, a method that excites children in the area of literacy and has children looking forward to coming into the classroom to share personal vocabulary is a method vital to any classroom. Furthermore, it keeps me excited about the insight I gain into the children's lives by simply asking, "What word would you like to learn today?", "What made you choose that word?" and then, "Now let's see how it looks in print." The conversation continues around the table as the children work on their Keywords, throughout the day with their Keyword hats, and then in the home as their Keywords accompany them to the family setting.

## NOTES

1. Sylvia Ashton-Warner, *Teacher* (New York: Simon & Schuster, 1963): 14.
2. Ibid, 46.
3. Ibid, 27.
4. Imagine It! Reading Program. New York: McGraw Hill Reading Program, (2007): accessed January 28, 2012. http://www.imagineitreading.com/NA/ENG_US/index.php
5. Ashton-Warner, *Teacher*, 47.
6. Ibid, 63.
7. Ibid, 32.
8. Ibid, 40.
9. Lee, Clara. "The mathematics of language acquisition," (2007): accessed April 10, 2008, http://arstenchica.com/journals/science.ars/2007/08/02/the-mathematics-of-language-acquisition.
10. Ibid, 3.
11. Ibid, 10.

## *Chapter 6*
## Keywords in a Second Grade Classroom

Teacher, looking up from the table: *Good Morning Shelia. How are you this morning?*
Shelia, a second grader, coming around to stand near teacher, answers in a quiet voice: *Fine.*
Teacher: *What word do you have on your mind today?*
Shelia already knows what her Keyword is going to be today. I can tell by her eyes she has been thinking about her word for some time and has been anticipating the moment she would able to finally share her word.
Shelia: *Buried*
Teacher: *Berry? Like strawberries or blueberries? I love strawberries.*
Shelia: *No, buried like in a box.*

As Shelia's second grade teacher, I repeat the word, "buried," take out an index card and marker, and write the word as I am saying the word aloud, confirming I have now heard the word correctly. Next, I punch a hole in the top corner of the index card and hand the word back to her.

Teacher: *Shelia, why are you thinking about the word 'buried' today?*
Shelia: *Over the weekend, my aunt's baby died, I got to see it in black and white then they put it in the box and buried it.*
Teacher: *Did you attend the funeral?*
Shelia: *Yes.*
Teacher: *Can you tell me a little more about seeing the baby in black and white?*

Shelia begins describing the hospital room and the screen where she could see the baby's picture while the baby was still inside the mother's womb.

Teacher: *Shelia, it sounds like you saw a sonogram of the baby.*
Shelia: *Oh.*
Teacher: *Shelia, could you write about your Keyword in a sentence?*

I then hand her a sentence strip, precut in half, and she heads back to her seat with her modeled word to write her sentence. Other students are at the Keywords table listening to our conversation and anxiously awaiting their turn to share their Keyword. Students move to and from the table fluidly as they arrive for the day, get their Keyword, and return to the table to share.

I continue through the same process with each child who visits the table. As the children listen to each other's words and descriptions, conversations begin amongst the children. They become excited about hearing the words and stories their classmates are sharing.

As Shelia finishes her sentence, she returns to the table. Her sentence strip reads, "*We buried the baby because it died at the house spilltlle and I saw the tiny baby in the coler black and white witheout no body in me.*" [We buried the baby because it died at the hospital and I saw the tiny baby in the color black and white, without anybody helping me.] She began to read her sentence aloud to me, well aware of the other students at the table listening.

As we discussed her work, Shelia further interpreted her sentence. Her aunt, who lived in the home, had indeed suffered the loss of a baby over the weekend. Shelia had seen the tiny baby in the black and white sonogram photo without anybody telling her where to look, whereas some family members had difficulty interpreting the photo.

This example proves just how profound Keywords can be for children and their teachers. The practice provides children a print outlet for expressing their lives, imaginations, and experiences. It allows an opening for them to express their own thinking and to use this thinking in a way that is meaningful for them. I am quite sure that without the forum of Keywords, Shelia could have gone through her entire day without having the chance to talk about this sad, but important, event with me. I would have proceeded with my reading, writing, math, etc. without her having a chance to discuss what was really on her mind. It also gave her a "safe space" to talk about a very powerful event with a trusted adult.

## WHY DOES THE KEYWORDS METHODOLOGY WORK?

I began my teaching internship in a second grade classroom, working in a Title One school with a population of students that were economically and socially disadvantaged. The school had begun piloting the Reading First program funded through the No Child Left Behind initiative of 2001[1]. With the implementation of NCLB in 2004, vocabulary instruction was back in the spotlight. Vocabulary, being one of the five components of reading, as declared by the National Reading Panel[2], was now being taught explicitly and systematically during literacy blocks in addition to reading comprehension and other components of literacy instruction. Questions had arisen from this mandate as to what were the most appropriate way to teach vocabulary acquisition. With this being my first classroom experience in literacy education,

I felt my own novice philosophy of literacy did not match the philosophy of Reading First nor its mandates for literacy instruction, but I was willing to give it a chance.

Although I used this time during my teaching internship to ask questions and explore other opportunities for literacy instruction, I was required to teach reading under the strict guidelines of Reading First. I was bound to teach using a basal reading series, spelling lists, protected blocks of time for phonics instruction, phonemic awareness, and other curricula from the five components of reading identified in NCLB. The reading block was designed to be systematic, much like the teaching of vocabulary. There was no time allotted for students to acquire or question words that sparked their curiosity or emotions. Still I questioned: should vocabulary words be given on a spelling list, based on phonics, or themes? Should they be teacher-selected, or student-selected?

As my internship came to an end, I accepted a teaching position in a second grade classroom at the same school. Some may ask, "Why would I not have explored other options considering my own personal philosophy of teaching did not align with Reading First?" I too struggled with this question when the job was offered to me, but not for long. It was a job and I was enthusiastic about doing my best. I knew this was an opportunity for me to become a versatile, effective teacher and saw it as a challenge to find other ways to supplement literacy instruction for a group of students who needed it most. I knew this group of students needed more than what Reading First offered, and I felt it was my responsibility to bring these additional experiences into the classroom.

It was not until my first full year of teaching that I began to see the effects of Reading First on literacy instruction. I believed the program was based on current research at the time and was focused around the five components of reading, but I came to fully understand that teaching was not a one-size-fits-all practice. I knew I needed more experience, more strategies and resources, and other teachers with whom to collaborate. I soon began graduate work in language and literacy. During this program, I began forming my own philosophy in the teaching of literacy and the acquisition of language. I was introduced to Sylvia Ashton-Warner and the vocabulary strategy she called Key Vocabulary. The vocabulary strategy allowed students to self-select words that were meaningful for them and to express these words in a meaningful context. Ashton-Warner describes these keywords as "organic" or "words that are already part of a child's being.[3]"

Through my own personal struggles, with working in a Reading First school, I began to see how this vocabulary strategy called Keywords. I immediately took interest in how I could adapt his instructional approach and make it function successfully in my own second grade classroom. To try it out, I began using the Keywords strategy as described by Ashton-Warner in the book, Teacher, with a first grader in an after-school tutoring setting. This is where I truly saw for myself the effectiveness of the Key Vocabulary methodology. I was able to envision how and when I could use this technique in my own classroom, and I began to develop a rationale for implementing it in the 2nd grade classroom. My second year of teaching, I began implementing what my students and I came to call *Keywords.* I have and will continue to use Keywords in my classroom when working with lower elementary students from kindergarten through fifth grade.

When determining how I could modify Keywords to fit my grade level, I began thinking about the objectives I was required to teach. Reading First monopolized the majority of my day with reading instruction and did not allow me to teach writing strategies, grammar, oral language, or sentence structure. I knew I needed a way to incorporate these skills into my reading instruction and continue to assess my students writing skills. I decided I would allow students to choose a Keyword daily and write their word in a sentence of their own design. This would allow me to incorporate and assess writing skills while allowing students to express their interests through the use of Keywords. It would be an opportunity for students to take control over their own learning. They would use their own word within the context of their own language. I designed a Keywords pocket chart to allow students to display their sentences for others to read and enjoy. They also revisited and reread their sentences throughout the day, both for the feeling of success it bred and as a reference for other writing activities. Children collected their Keywords on metal rings, which were kept in the classroom. I had a wooden strip with hooks installed on the wall just under the white board where students would hang their Keywords for easy access. I allowed students to take home their Keyword rings after each nine weeks so these could be shared with family and friends. At that time they would begin a new Keyword ring.

## WHAT ARE THE BENEFITS OF KEYWORDS?

I had to think about how I would pitch this activity to the students to gain the most interest. I knew this was an activity that I did not want to impose on the children. I wanted it to be optional so students never felt forced, but I knew the opportunity for a word would be there if they chose to share. I also knew I wanted to maintain high expectations for writing samples without taking away from the enjoyment and excitement of using their Keywords in their own sentences. I started with skills students should have mastered in first grade, expecting students to have capital letters at the beginning of sentences and beginning of names, punctuation marks at the end of sentences, and proper sentence structure. I wanted students to know this was a chance to show everyone how exceptional their writing could be and to tell a story about their Keywords. As the year progressed, I began looking for the new writing and grammar skills I had taught to be reflected in their Keyword sentences, and I continued to hold these high expectations for their writing throughout the year.

During the Keywords activity, I checked for their understanding of the word and how they used it within the context of the sentence. I also used this opportunity to check for the correct spelling of the Keyword as well as for high frequency and core words. I looked for adjectives, appropriate capitalization, and punctuation, and made note of a child's progress. This is a quick way to informally assess grammatical competence and how students were doing with expressive writing. I made a point to find something positive to say about the sentence, whether it was pointing out an adjective, the correct use of an exclamation mark, or how I heard their author's voice coming through their writing.

In my classroom I wanted children to use Keywords to enhance their sight word fluency. This strategy allowed for daily oral practice and gave students the opportunity to create their own sight word lists, as the words were collected on rings and reread daily as they visited the Keyword table. Some students chose to reread their Keywords before getting a new word while other students may get a new word and later reread their other words when adding their new Keyword to their ring. I tried to leave the process open to each student's preference and to maintain the theme of choice throughout implementation. For me, Keywords became more of a methodology. It was no longer just a literacy strategy, but a change in beliefs about literacy for my children and me.

## How does the Keywords Methodology look in a second grade classroom?

I used Keywords in the morning as a rotational morning activity to get children focused and excited about the day. It also allowed me a few minutes to check in with the children before the school day begins. I opened the Keywords table at 7:30 a.m. as the first students are arriving in the classroom. Morning work was already on the board and the students choose whether to visit the Keywords table first and then complete morning work or to complete morning work and then visit with me at the Keywords table. Keywords was always an optional activity and is never forced upon the students. When students came to the table I have a bucket of materials in the center of the table. I had blank index cards, a paper hole puncher, markers, and sentence strips cut in half. It is important to have these materials together and available so Keywords can start quickly. If I have run out of any materials I replenish them each afternoon. I used the plastic tub to keep the materials organized and accessible during the Keywords time. Their word rings hung nearby and the sentence strip pocket chart hung on the board just above, near the Keywords table.

After the student shared their sentence with me and the other people at the Keywords table, the student then puts their sentence on the Keywords pocket chart for the remainder of the day. Other students could read the sentences as they added their own sentences to the pocket chart. The students then put their new Keyword on their Keyword ring, reread the Keywords already on their ring, and put their ring back on the hook. Students knew they could revisit their Keywords at any time during writing, spelling, or reading activities. Students left their seats or work stations to get their words and returned them when they were finished.

I usually closed down the Keywords table at 8:10 a.m., or about 40 minutes into the school day. This typically allowed all children who chose to participate that day to visit with me. As I stated before, Keywords was an optional activity left up to the student's choice in my classroom. This was a completely student-centered activity, which I did not impose on any students. Some students chose to visit every day, others two or three times a week, some only a few times a month, and one or two preferred to listen but not partake in the written component of the activity. Students accumulated their Keywords for nine weeks.

At the end of the nine weeks, we had a Keywords Share Day when students sat with a partner or in groups of three and shared their Keywords and experiences. Some children had accumulated nearly forty words by this point while others may only have had fifteen or twenty word cards. These sharing sessions usually took between twenty and thirty minutes, allowing time for word reading and student conversation. Words you might hear during these sharing sessions varied greatly. Some word rings included names of family and friends, different types of animals, places traveled, television shows and characters, as well as movie titles and toys. This was always an exciting time full of stories, word reading, and enthusiasm. The children who took part in this activity ranged from students identified with special needs participating through inclusion, general education students, and academically gifted students. Regardless of the students' academic standings, Keywords provided commonality for them all and a time for them to feel successful, proud, and intelligent.

## WHY PRACTICE KEYWORDS? WHAT RATIONALE DOES RESEARCH PROVIDE?

Brabham and Villaume continue to inspire me with their statement, "Our greatest challenge is to become spirited teachers who are captivated by words and delighted by the insights that are revealed as we lead students to wonder about the words of our language.[4]" As a teacher of language and literacy, this encompasses the meaning and the value of using this strategy with my students. I want to find ways to inspire creativity and curiosity about language and give students an avenue to explore their own literacy. I can only hope my engagement and enthusiasm for Keywords will ignite a passion within my students that will foster a love for language and literacy.

When considering the value of Keywords, we can look to others who have read the work of Sylvia Ashton-Warner and have used this strategy in their own classrooms. Nancy Thompson paraphrases Ashton-Warner by saying, "her insight was that the words children speak out of the emotional lives are accompanied by vivid mental images.[5]" When I think about Shelia and her Keyword "buried," the vivid imagery attached to that word also attaches to its meaning. To her, Keywords is an outlet, an opportunity to share meaning and an attempt to give another person a glimpse of the vivid image she had in her mind. Keywords may have been the only way Shelia could share this experience. There are not many other opportunities during the school day to discuss topics such as death or funerals, but Shelia knew on Monday morning she could count on the opportunity to talk about her Keyword in a safe environment.

Carolyn Mamchur wrote about her own teaching experiences derived from the work of Sylvia Ashton-Warner; "The essence of the organic method is that it touches those things very deep and real within a child.[6]" Thinking back once more to Shelia and her Keyword "buried," this word held an intense and real meaning for her, as do the Keywords of other children choosing to participate in this activity.

Keywords is a truly motivating strategy that allows students to take ownership over their learning. Students often do not comprehend new vocabulary words because they have no connection to the word's meaning. Words become dull and students disinterested in learning new vocabulary. From birth through adulthood, children learn approximately eight new words daily with a slight increase between the ages of two and five[7]. This astounding evidence of the capabilities of children to acquire words connects with the ability of my second graders to daily add new written words to their sight vocabulary. Why should children not be trusted with the daily opportunity to add new words with significance to their written vocabulary? Brabham and Villaume said, "A rich vocabulary is fired by a fascination with language that creates disposition and motivation for learning words.[8]" Children need to feel connected to their learning, and Keywords can be an integral part in the learning community.

## NOTES

1. U.S. Department of Education, "Executive Summary of the No Child Left Behind Act of 2001": accessed January 28, 2012, http://www2.ed.gov/nclb/overview/intro/execsumm.html

2. International Reading Association's Summary of National Reading Panel Report: accessed April 10, 2008, http://www.reading.org/resources/issues/reports/nrp.html

3. Sylvia Ashton-Warner, *Teacher* (New York: Simon & Schuster, 1963): 32.

4. Edna Brabham and Susan Villaume, "Vocabulary instruction: Concerns and visions," *The Reading Teacher* 56, (2002): 267.

5 Nancy Thompson, "Sylvia Ashton-Warner: Reclaiming Personal Meaning in Literacy Teaching," *The English Journal* 89, no. 3 (2000).

6. Carolyn Mamchur. "Heart Beat," *Educational Leadership* 40, no. 4 (1983): 20.20.

7. Clara Lee, "The mathematics of language acquisition," (2007): accessed April 10, 2008, http://arstenchica.com/journals/science.ars/2007/08/02/the-mathematics-of-language-acquisition.

8. Brabham and Villaume, 265.

## *Chapter 7*
## Keywords for English Language Learners

Ashton-Warner's words were first introduced to me in my own teacher education program in the late 1970's. After my first teaching experiences as a Peace Corps Volunteer in Lesotho, I saw first-hand the importance of a child's connection with text. Back in the United States as a HeadStart Preschool teacher, I worked almost exclusively with children whose families spoke Spanish as the home language, with varying degrees of fluency in English as their second language. Our objective was to give literacy experiences in the classroom that could then carry over to home literacy practices. This included Spanish and English songs, rhymes, finger plays and stories, some of which HeadStart staff and parents shared. For my predominantly Spanish speaking 4 year olds, as stated previously in Chapter 3, I saw the need for my curriculum to have meaningful connections about culturally relevant topics. I particularly looked for this in vocabulary that would crossover conceptually in both languages, such as Mommy and Mama, or in a song where baby chicks sang "Peep-peep!" much like the "*pío-pío*" of *pollitos* (chicks). If I were to choose one word that had both school and home significance for the children it would have been "bike". Since there were only 4 bikes for the 20 or so children, the word was used to negotiate turns, express a need, and create a bond between children as they played together. The word seemed to ring in my ears each day on the playground, yet I don't remember it having significance in print in the classroom. I had not yet made the connection of Ashton-Warner's work from playground to the Keywords table.

My first public school job was as a kindergarten teacher in Oxnard, California, again teaching children whose language and culture was different from my own and from what was represented in the reading texts. Most of my students spoke a mixture of English and Spanish, and easily code-switched between the two languages. Most of the children in my classroom lived in extended and blended family groups in apartment buildings. The stories I overheard in the dramatic play center or in the sandbox on the playground included large family events and traditions. Their "play-talk" was rich in what

Ashton-Warner called intimate words, full of caring terms, names of siblings, and family scenes. I saw many of the girls play in the playhouse, singing lullabies to dollies and cooking pretend tacos. Boys too dramatized family events, particularly in the block area, building houses and driving block vehicles down imaginary roads. They talked about animals different from the urban domesticated pets, such as cats and dogs, or more exotic zoo animals, often used in children's texts. Many of them visited relatives in Mexico during the winter holiday season; therefore, *chivos* (goats), *toros* (bulls) and *culebras* (snakes), representing powerful and very present animals, were used in oral stories and play. Likewise, their free form artwork showed intimate scenes in homes, parks and community sites, such as church and sport games. However their everyday lives as represented in play were missing from their written texts when it came to scripted reading and writing programs.

The need for Keywords in my classroom became clear...when a child's own personal text were connected to classroom text it inspired attention to that text. It provided an opportunity to talk about the "word"—grammatically, phonologically, and semantically. In this way I could introduce language rules in an individual context, which is often difficult to do in a multilingual setting, such as a whole class modeled writing lesson or classroom read-aloud. For instance, a second language acquirer might ask for a Keyword, such as "Arthur", but pronounce the word as "Artur". Because the /th/ sound is not used in Spanish this gave me, the teacher, a prime opportunity to teach the letter-sound combination in a meaningful context, as I wrote the /th/ on the card.

Having a personal conversation with me at the Keyword table stemming from the chosen word of the day was also clearly a way for me to connect culturally with the individual child's home and interests. At the same time, it provided a situation for the children to connect their words, as they participated in sidebar conversations about their words, while they waited for their turn or worked on their Keyword hat. All of these learning opportunities happened naturally in and across both languages. The Keyword table was a multilingual space. Children used their language of choice, with me as a second language learner also participating in the language acquisition process.

In the following twenty-one years, with different grade levels, age groups, and language and culture mixes, I used Keywords with every group and with always the same gusto. I used the methods with kindergarten/1$^{st}$ grade combination class that was designed as a dual immersion program. In this classroom configuration my class included kindergarteners of one home language (English or Spanish in our region) and a first grade group of the other home language (Spanish or English). The kindergarteners looped, or stayed with me as their teacher, so that they became my first graders the following year, with the home language of the new kindergartners changing to be the opposite of the returning first graders. The two grade levels naturally code-switched between languages throughout the day, exposing each other to the conversational nature of natural second language acquisition. As the teacher, I used the home language of the child as the instructional language, but did not stop them from using their new second language as it immerged. This also occurred at the Keyword table. For instance, if a Kindergartener (English dominant, let's say), requested the word, "goat", for her Keyword, then it was natural for the Spanish speaking 1st graders sitting around the table to discuss and "play with" the word, translating it for each other..."Goat! The Three Billy Goats Gruff. Los chivos quieren cruzar el puente. Uhmmmmm (making horns and movements like a ram." As I wrote and discussed the word "goat" for the kindergartener's new word, the other children around the table, including first graders, observed and sometimes participated in our conversation about the word, adding it to their concept of the word in their first language and the vocabulary bank of their second language.

Language acquisition theories state that second language exposure contributes to the first language lexicon, as the child constructs knowledge and critically assimilates this concept semantically, syntactically and phonologically in the first language.[1]

With Keywords children are exposed to second language vocabulary through their peers' choices of words, as well as the discussion around their own words. Often times a child's first attempts in independently using the new 2nd language occurred at the Keyword table. This might be in the name of a new friend or a concept introduced in class. This occurred in a Kindergarten class where I recently observed Keywords in action. The teacher's bulletin board showed photographs of penguins and maps. A non-fiction big-book on penguins sat on the easel. A copy of Tacky the Penguin[2] was front and center on the book rack. As I reviewed the Keyword pocket chart I could see that children from both home language groups present in this classroom (Spanish and English) had multiple Keywords on the topic, i.e. pinguino, penguin, pouch, huevo, egg. The teacher commented that the children loved their current science unit on polar climates, including penguins. This was reflected in the words they chose to learn to write for Keywords.

In my own classroom I reflected how this view into the language interests of a 2nd language learner provided information about the grammar and pronunciation skills of the child, as they often approximated the pronunciation of the word. In the example above of the word, "Arthur", pronounced as "Artur", I was able to teach this letter-sound combination in a meaningful context. Over the years I had multiple chances to discuss the letter-sound relationship of /j/ with English speaking children in writing their Keywords, as they chose their friends' names—Jose, Jesus, Josefina, Jasmin. These conversations went something like this: *In English we say, /j-j-j-Joey, but in Spanish we say /h/h/hos-e"*. Children learned that letter-sound relationships were dynamic and flexible—drawing interest to the idea of both first and second languages. Research supports this "learning about language" as a part of the natural acquisition of a second language.[3]

The benefits of keywords as a second language methodology were clear to see when I used it to teach English as a Second Language to adult students in a community college setting. The students in these non-credit classes hoped to learn English at a successful level to enable them to eventually enroll in credit course. The students came from multiple language backgrounds—Hmong, Hungarian & Spanish, Portuguese, etc. We began each class in much the same way I opened my elementary classes…as the adult students entered the college classroom they sat down at the Keyword table, their Keyword envelope full of past Keywords ready for sharing. Before getting a new keyword, the adult student read and briefly defined their Keyword collection, such as "record—it's like for music, pencil—it's for—um-m-m--writing; table-it's what we sit at for writing or eating". Then, answering a simple request, much like that I used with my small learners, I asked: "What word do you want to learn to write in English today?" The adult students sometimes entered the room with a word they'd been "saving" to have translated for their new Keyword. As with small children, these words often linked to concepts important in the learner's life, such as "manejar" (to drive) or "applicar" (to apply). Other times they chose words from the classroom environment, wanting to see a familiar object translated into English. Other times they were curious to see how a spoken word they had acquired in English would look in print. I particularly remember a student who wanted the word "chair" because he could not find it in the dictionary when he had tried to spell it the way he was pronouncing it (with a soft /ch/), except as the name of a famous American entertainer or the verb meaning to allow others to use or partake. Modeling the pronunciation and spelling, and then clarifying the irregular vowel combination, were "in-context" opportunities to talk about sound-symbol relationships as well as homophones. As the remainder of the group listened in on the mini-lesson the group then repeated the new word in unison, an ESL technique that builds confidence for new second language speakers. The student then copied the Keyword on a list kept in a notebook full of this and other vocabulary exercises that went home with the student. Students often copied each other's keywords into their notebooks as we progressed around the table. This practice was so interactive and meaningful to the students that we allowed 30-45 minutes of the 2 hour evening class period so that every student could gain a new Keyword at each class.

For more than twenty years I taught Kindergarten, 1st and 2nd grades, with multiple languages in the same classroom, and adult English as a Second Language students in a community college setting. Among these different ages, needs and abilities Keywords has been the most popular and active center in my classroom. It is also the activity that, once introduced, children can't seem to live without during their school day. They are ready with a new Keyword as the classroom day begins. They are truly disappointed when it is interrupted or not provided. As I now observe teachers in current classrooms I see Keywords having the same effect on second language learners; it improves attention to text, it provides a forum for discussing the properties of a word, and it gives a situational context to talk with each student—no matter what age—about what she or he wants to learn to write that day—in whatever language available.

## NOTES

1. Jim Cummins. "Language proficiency, biliteracy and French immersion," *Canadian Journal of Linguistics* 8, no. 2. (1983): 117-138.

2. Helen Lester, Tacky the Penguin. (New York: Houghton Mifflin).

3.Monique Bournot-Trites and Ulrike Tellowitz, "Report of Second Language Learning on First Language Literacy Skills". (Halifax, Nova Scotia: The Atlantic Provinces Educational Foundation) 2002: 11-20. Accessed January 26, 2012, http:www.edina.k12.mn.us/normandale/media/weblinks/teachers/pdfs/report1.pdf.

# *Chapter 8*
# Adaptations to Fit Other Classroom Contexts

> *I like talking about keywords with my teacher.*
>
> *I love keywords becaces (because) you get to wirte (write) some sentence and you get to pit (put) up your keyword and the bet (best) one is you get to spen (spend) time with your lovele thcer (lovely teacher).*

The role of focused conversation in building a relationship between the child, the teacher and the word that Keywords inspires cannot be underestimated, as expressed by the two children in the above vignette. Giving voice to a child's inner world is no less important in a special education classroom, a remedial reading tutoring session, or a pull-out ESL program than in a traditional self-contained classroom. As has always been the case, the Keyword methodology has been modified to fit the age and setting of the participating children and adults. However, following are a few examples of how teachers have made the method of response to the teacher's prompt fit their particular setting. First, Sarah will describe her Keyword methodology as seen in a Special Education classroom setting. Next, Amy will describe adaptations she made for Keywords in her second grade classroom. Thirdly, Keywords will be described when adapted for preschool children, upper elementary and middle school students in an afterschool tutoring setting.

## Sarah's Story

The rationale of Keywords in my classroom relates to communication between the student, teacher, home, and peers. For most students in my program, it is difficult to simply answer the question, "*What word* do you want to write today?" Answering a simple "what" question can be confusing for some students, and "word" is too abstract for many students. Also, it is difficult to get true meaning from some student responses because they will oftentimes repeat what I say or what another student says. However, Keywords clearly builds verbal comprehension by making connections between their school day and their writing (i.e., "toy center" or "Daddy").

Keywords allow me to differentiate instruction for each student without additional preparation. Simply asking a child what word they want to write is sometimes too abstract for students with disabilities or delays. I have used physical options to suggest a word, such as pointing to objects around the room. I have also used picture cards to help a child choose a word to write. If a child was non-verbal she or he told me the word they wanted to write through other means. This could be through signing, pointing or gesturing. One child in my class who is wheel chair bound and non-verbal, has a collection of Keywords, all named by eye-gaze and facial expressions to indicate a word she wanted to use as I named words for her to choose from. For example, I have an alphabet chart with pictures and I can point to an object on the chart. She will gesture and show excitement when I choose a word she wants for a Keyword from the chart. Likewise, she will give me a flat response on words in which she has no interest. True joy lit up her face each day as we discovered together the word she wanted to see me write for her. Although it took some guessing, she was clear that she had the time and patience to give me until I named the word she was indicating for her Keyword choice.

In other cases, due to speech articulation issues, I have researched in order to make sure I had the correct word the child wanted to write, i.e., asked a parent to translate, asked questions to child and then look up options on the internet, etc. At times other children in my classroom have helped me to understand the Keyword a child is expressing. All of these methods have helped to ensure that I am listening correctly to the child.

The way in which a child completed their Keyword practice in my classroom depended on the child. Since my class was made up of a variety of ability descriptions, some students only traced a word with hand-over-hand assistance. For another child, I wrote the word card as well as the word in multiple colors on the hat band, encouraging the child to watch me do the repetitive writing. Others wrote the word, formulated and illustrated their sentence. In all cases the sentence strip was stapled to make a hat for the child to show their Keyword to others.

In my class I do not send the word cards home, but instead, depending on the child we read the words together or the child reads the words independently each day before getting a new word. This review helped not only the child whose words we read but also the other children around the room, as they learned to recognize the Keywords of their peers. Often the child does not know the previous day's Keyword in an EC classroom. I simply tell them the Keyword again, have them take a mental picture of the written word, and we move on.

The hat was sent home each day, giving the child something to share with their parents. For parents and caregivers it provided a connection between something their child did at school and then retelling or showing it at home. This is especially important for families of non-verbal and less communicative children, who are sometimes less able to understand the workings of the school day.

Not always did every child do a Keyword every day. School demands and the class roster for a given year determined how often and for how many minutes a day I was able to do Keywords. In some school years we scheduled Keywords in our small group/self-contained setting every day with every child. This school year we practiced Keywords twice a week. Since Keywords were scheduled for every student, the children don't see it as an optional activity. Wearing the Keyword hat was an additional incentive for them to complete the activity, besides having focused one-on-one teacher time.

This year we practiced Keyword writing during our scheduled writing block, just before lunch. The children had the option to wear their Keyword hat to the cafeteria, which they almost always did.

I kept my Keywords cards organized with a hole punch, which I added the child's new Keyword to their own Keyword ring each day. These were hung on a pegboard that was kept in clear sight of the child and made available for them to look at for both a resource and/or for a classroom activity—to simply read the Keywords. This success oriented activity was often chosen by my children during their center time.

In my small classroom, I have found that Keywords can be incorporated into the school day at the child's request when they ask for something to be added to their Keyword ring. Children initiated the incorporation by choosing a word that related to something that just happened at school or something that anticipated would occur that school day. *Teacher, can I make a Keyword hat out of that word?* In a larger classroom I might not have had the freedom to do so, but in my setting, I can seize the teachable moment and say *Yes!* to putting the child's word in print.

## AMY'S STORY

In my classroom the morning is the best time for Keywords because the child has the opportunity to use and refer to the word throughout the entire school day. Every child does a Keyword every day. I begin our small group instruction with Keywords. The children's word cards are organized in their individual "Word Bags" and they bring them to me at our small group table, ready to begin the session. As the bag grows, the words are transferred to a ring. I keep blank cards and other materials organized in my own Word Bag. Children can retrieve this bag for me when we need to add a Keyword during another part of the day, as sometimes spontaneously occurs.

The children read the words collected in their Word Bag to the small group before getting a new word. Children use sentence strips to write their word repeatedly, or they may use the sentence strip to write a sentence using the word. Some children like the more "grown up" version of using an index card to write the word and a definition as their take home Keyword.

If the child does not know the previous day's Keyword I simply have them review it with them and then put it back in their Word Bags to continue to revisit. This then becomes a word to which we will continue to pay more attention. I don't hesitate to help them with their words as needed.

I have children keep their Keywords all year rather than taking them home. Their rings become full of words that then become a reference to use constantly and consistently throughout the year in writing and other ways. The cards are then sent home at the conclusion of the year.

I see Keywords as a part of building vocabulary, one of the essential components of literacy. I am easily able to fit it into our class schedule by building it into my daily small group instruction. I have never had a parent, principal or colleague challenge this use of the school day.

## In a Preschool Setting

As a preschool teacher at an accredited childcare education center, I believed strongly in emergent literacy at its own pace and purpose. Therefore Keywords needed to be modified to appropriately fit the needs of a pre-emergent and emergent level of literacy. In this setting Keywords was a modeled writing activity that incorporated the 3 and 4 year olds' oral language. Our preschool was situated at a community college. A diverse group of children attended, some whose parent was attending college in either credit or non-credit classes, and others whose parent(s) were faculty members. This interesting collage of family diversity contributed to a mix of literacy backgrounds for the children, not separated necessarily by economics or education level only but also by lifestyles. In the center, the 3 and 4 year olds had an array of activities to choose from, all designed by age appropriate practice guidelines. One thirty minute period of the day children were grouped by language and math ability to participate in a structured lesson. Not all children were ready for keywords, but for those who were, It was an oral language activity.

When the group of ten or twelve children sat down in a circle around the teacher, she would have a whiteboard easel and markers ready. The teacher asked, "Who has a word to tell us about today?" Logan might raise his hand, an action requesting a turn to talk, used only in this circle time. "I want 'train'!" "Train" the teacher repeats. "Tell us about train. What do you know about a train?" Logan proceeds to tell the group about the train he could see in the morning coming to school...how a stick had come down to tell all the cars to stop. His mom was the first car to stop and so he could see all the train cars go by. His mom told him that some of the cars had cars inside and others might have food or toys." The teacher asks, "Has anyone else seen the train that Logan is talking about?" After a brief story time with other children connecting to Logan's idea of the train, the teacher says, "Okay, let's look at Logan's word on paper." She then writes the word on the chart paper, discussing the letters as she writes. "Is there anyone here who has the same letter as train at the beginning of their name?" The preschoolers have multiple versions of their name printed around the center, in their cubby, on their sleeping mat, on their blankets, so many do recognize not only their own names but that of other children. the teacher finishes Logan's word with a sketch or simple drawing alongside his word. This mnemonic device will help Logan and others make a further connection...that not only with letters but with other types of symbols can represent the concept of train. The teacher continues the activity, asking for other children to name a keyword that they would like to share. The chart paper is hung in the classroom where parents can see it as they pick up their child. Logan might share the word with his mom, pointing it out, The modeling of writing and drawing to represent the spoken word naturally transitioned for many of the children to copying the words and pictures on to their own paper during free time. The speaking, listening and turn taking of Keyword Circle time was also a valuable element of the methodology for this age, as it built on their own language and interests, modeling the importance of constructing knowledge from not only teachers but also their peers.

## IN AN AFTERSCHOOL TUTORING SETTING

Being an early elementary teacher for a number of years, Amy took on the challenge of tutoring upper elementary students who were struggling in reading and writing as a part of a graduate assignment. In this class Keywords had been described as a way to build early concepts of print, but also to reinforce spoken vocabulary. The school at which Amy taught had a richly diverse student and faculty population. The entire fifth grade class was learning about World War II. Amy, having traveled to Japan in the recent summer, shared her experiences with the two 5th grade girls during their tutoring sessions. Together they previewed the chapter book being read in their regular class each day. Keywords became a part of the support strategy for their reading. The girls read silently from the book, a page at a time, and then discussed the page between themselves and Amy. They then chose a word from the text for their novel keyword.

Amy reported the girls recorded their Keywords in a journal made especially for this purpose. They selected the word, the three then discussed its meaning in the context of the story and then looked up the definition in a dictionary she had on hand for that purpose. In their journals they wrote the page number the word is found in the book, they write the official definition. They sometimes chose on their own to sketch the word or write more about it from the context of the story.

Occasionally the girls came into the tutoring session asking Amy to do Keywords before reading and outside of the context of their chapter book. The first time this happened it seemed spontaneous and Amy was a little surprised. This often happened with her 2$^{nd}$ graders, but not with the more guarded older girls. What she learned however was that the organic nature of the vocabulary was just as relevant for these eleven year olds as the seven and eight year olds. Darlene's (pseudonym) Keyword that first day was "diabetes." In this way she shared with her best friend—the other tutee—and Amy the details of her disease. Both Shawn (pseudonym) and Amy were aware of Darlene's diabetes, but they had never had a forum to discuss it. By adding it to her Keyword journal, she was able to read and copy the official definition according to the elementary level dictionary. She also wrote descriptive sentences about it from her context. Keywords continued to be a practice for the two girls that made both text-to-text as well as text-to-life connections.

This same adaptation was used in a middle school tutoring session. Here the teacher/tutor read side by side with the 9$^{th}$ grade girl, each taking a turn to tease apart the story. The teacher, having previously made the arrangement with the regular classroom teacher, knew what chapter or section of the book would be read on the following day, and used the tutoring hour to preview it with the student. Much like in Amy's tutoring, a Keyword Journal was used to record a word from the text that appeared either interesting, or perhaps difficult, and needed more attention. In this instance, the tutor also chose a word to add to the student's journal, making two new entries a day. The definition was recorded, as well as the sentence in which the word was found in the book. These were reviewed on a regular basis, adding to the student's understanding of the text as well as building her sight vocabulary.

When asked at the end of the ten week tutoring session, both the 9$^{th}$ grade student and the tutor considered the Keyword Journal to be one of the most effective and pleasurable elements of the session.

In these examples the role of focused conversation in building a relationship between the child, the teacher and the word that Keywords inspired could not be replaced by a predetermined vocabulary list or writing prompt. Giving voice to a child's inner world is no less important in a special education classroom, a remedial reading tutoring session, or a pull-out ESL program than in a traditional classroom. The Keyword methodology, when modified, can fit the age and setting of the participating children and young adults.

*Chapter 9*

# How to Easily and Effectively Set Up Your Classroom for Keywords

In my own practice I set up my Keywords program much as Ashton-Warner did in the classroom she described in *Teacher*. Each afternoon before closing my classroom door for the day I liked to set up my Keyword table. In that way I could make sure that no matter what else interrupted my morning prep time I would have Keywords ready to go when the children arrived. I devoted approximately 20 instructional minutes of my morning to the Keyword table. As not all children were able to get their word of the day during that time I often opened the table up in the afternoon during Center Time as well. On the round or kidney shaped table I made ready markers, lined 3 x 5 index cards, sentence strips and a stapler. The Keywords table was always sitting in close proximity to the Keyword chart...a pocket chart with a library card sized pocket for each child's name. As the children arrived I would ask them if they wanted to do a keyword. As the children wandered in the table would fill. The keyword question that I consistently used was "What word do you want to learn to write today?" As one child would finish copying their word onto the sentence strip another would sit down. Within the first 20 minutes of the day 8-10 children would have a new Keyword.

In all the various classrooms examined here Keywords was implemented in similar but slightly modified ways. The descriptors that were consistent however were very important. A Keyword is a word of choice and is not influenced by what the teacher assumes is best for the child. Participating in Keywords is also is a choice. Children chose to come to the table, rather than being asked or assigned.

Keywords is best when done at the beginning of the day, although some of us found it important to offer at other times of the day as well, in order to give more children an opportunity to participate daily. In the school using a Direct Instruction program Keywords takes place in the 30 minutes prior to the implementation of the scripted curriculum.

In all examples the teacher sat at a table that becomes the Keyword space for that period of the day. The frequency of the children's participation can be tracked by the amount of stored words, as the word cards are kept in the classroom in all three cases. Melissa and Chelsey use a pocket chart with the pockets labeled by the children's names and Joy' has the $2^{nd}$ graders add their new word to their personal Keyword ring and hang it on a hook.

In all classrooms the children bring their word collections to the teacher table and quickly review their words before getting their new Keyword. This step is important as it empowers the children as readers...they own these words. As Melissa put it so well: "What truly amazes me is how right Sylvia Ashton-Warner was...they don't forget the words!" Analysis showed the kindergarten children in her class were able to recite between 95 to 100% of the total number of keywords in their pocket.

If a child did not remember the word in most cases the teacher prompted the child. Chelsey said she chose to do what Ashton-Warner described and destroy the word. She made what she called a difficult choice initially but now understands the rationale... "I have them review their words first before they get a new one. The special educational kids and the English Language Learners... they all do it. If they can't read it I throw it out...it's one less thing off their back." She says: "This is how I have made it work in my classroom. When my students enter the room and take care of their morning tasks, they can come to my table where I have materials ready to make their keyword of the day. I ask one or several students, *What word would you like to learn to read today?* By now, some children come into the room and have already thought of the word they want for their Keyword. Others need some time and do not come to the table until after they have worked on their morning work or at a center for a bit. There are those that won't want to learn a new word until tomorrow, and that is fine too." As in the case of Shelia, the $2^{nd}$ grader in Joy's classroom, the need to share the Keyword with a caring adult is made obvious when a child walks in with such an emotionally charged word.

Following is a list of *Frequently Asked Questions*, with responses included by the three teachers currently involved with Keywords. The responses are listed in order by grade level, with Melissa giving a response for Kindergarten, Chelsey's response for 1st grade and Joy's response for $2^{nd}$ grade.

## FREQUENTLY ASKED QUESTIONS

1. What time of the day is best to do Keywords?

Melissa: I find first thing in the morning to be the best time of day to do Keywords; however, I may also do them during our writing block or reading groups as well.

Chelsey: I open the Keywords table as soon as the students are finished unpacking in the morning. It is a great way to check in with the children to catch any emotional needs and to just say good morning! Keywords is also available during literacy centers if children did not get a chance before instruction begins.

Joy: I prefer to begin first thing every morning as students arrive. This gives me the opportunity to check in with each child that chooses to get a Keyword that day. I think that sharing can take place anytime during the day. This gives students a chance to continue to revisit their words.

2. Does every child do a Keyword every day?

Melissa: No, not every child learns a word each day. Our time for morning work only lasts about 20 minutes and not all students are present at this time; therefore, I try to open the Keywords table at other times during the day. I would say that most children who want to learn a word typically come to the Keyword table three times each week. This is a voluntary activity and never forced.

Chelsey: I would also give each child the opportunity to do Keyword every day. Many times the table would become too crowded and I would have to select 8-10 for the morning and then reserve the rest during literacy centers.

Joy: Every child is given the daily opportunity to select a Keyword but not all will participate daily. Some choose to participate every other day, or a few time a week, while others may only select a word once a week. Participation is encouraged but never forced.

3. How do you organize the cards and other materials?

Melissa: I had a small basket with multi colored index cards, a hole puncher, stapler, permanent marker, and a few pencils. I also have a stack of multi colored sentence strips. The kids kept their Keywords on a key ring. They kept the key ring in their pencil box or in their chair pocket (the fabric chair cover in which they kept all their materials) at their seat.

Chelsey: I used library card envelopes, one for each child, attached to a large poster board that I would laminate. I would use a razor blade to cut an opening for each of the library card envelopes. Then I would label the library card envelopes with each child's name. At the Keywords table I would have a basket in the center of the round table that would contain index cards, markers, crayons, staplers, and a dictionary. I would also make sure that I had a good supply of sentence strips available at the table.

Joy: I have organized the cards in two different ways. I have used a row of hooks and chart paper rings as well as a pocket chart organizer. I prefer to use the rings and hooks because the rings hold many more cards without the chance of cards spilling out of the pocket and becoming confused with other students' cards. You could also use a Keywords journal for older students or students that may come to your classroom for a small group. For all other materials, I used a storage bin container which I filled with index cards, markers, a hole punch, sentence strips pre-cut in half, pencils, and extra rings. I kept this container on the table where I conducted Keywords and replenished supplies as needed.

4. How often do you send the Keyword cards home?

Melissa: I sent the Keywords home in groups of 10. Once the student has 11 words on his/her key ring, we leave the most recent word - the word they had learned that day—then take the remaining 10 and put them in the child's daily communication folder to go home that day. They get so excited about this and it is really funny watching them count their words to try to determine how many more they need before they can take them home—a very meaningful math lesson!

Chelsey: I sent the Keywords home at the end of each quarter. The students' pockets (where they stored their words) began to get too full at this point. Along with the words, I sent a letter home with the child explaining how the words were used in the classroom and how they could be practiced at home.

Joy: As you can see from the differing answers here that when to send the Keywords home is based on teacher or student preference. Just remember to stay consistent and continuously send the words home to continue building a home-school connection and encourage home sharing. I sent words home every quarter for my students.

5. How do you handle it if the child does not know the previous day's Keyword?

Melissa: This does not happen very often; however, it does sometimes occur at the beginning of the year in Kindergarten when students are just beginning to learn their letters and letter sounds. Typically the child gets mixed up and may mistake one Keyword for another. If this happens, I call their attention to the first letter of the word and remind them of that letter sound. From there, the child almost always remembers the word. If this happens repeatedly I may ask the child if he/she minds if I keep that word and we replace it with another the next day.

Chelsey: This only happened a few times. I asked the child if it was okay with them to get rid of the word they did not remember and they always wanted to get rid of the word. I felt that if the student did not remember the word, it was not important to them at that point in time. Therefore, keeping this word would make Keywords time an anxiety filled time, which was not what it was all about.

Joy: If a child does not know the Keyword I always take the opportunity to review the word and see if there was or still is any connection to the word. If so, I would encourage the student to keep the word for a day or two longer and then we would evaluate if we should get rid of the word or keep it. If the student showed no connection to the word initially or after a day or two then we would not keep the word.

6. What if a child wants an inappropriate word for her/his Keyword?

Melissa: This is a sensitive question which depends greatly on the teacher. Our students come from various walks of life and their own personal experiences may vary greatly from my own. What I may view as inappropriate may be a very real presence in the life of a child. Their vocabulary may contain words which I am completely unaware of the meaning of. In the case of an appropriate word I think it is the discussion with the child that is very important. Bottom line, as Joy said, the teacher needs to be prepared to justify the teaching practices in the classroom.

Chelsey: I was never faced with this situation; however, if this situation arose I would let the child know that this word is inappropriate and cannot be one of their Keywords. Depending on the age of the child, this word may be a word that is said loosely at home and the child does not realize the inappropriateness of the word. Of course there are those children that would want one of those words because they are attention seekers, but you would have the discussion about how this word should be a word that the child really has a passion for rather than for attention.

Joy: This is a sensitive question which I feel greatly depends on how the teacher defines inappropriate. Does the child want a curse word or a violent word such as kill? I always ask the child why they have chosen the word and we will discuss their reasons for doing so. Even if the word is too offensive to have in their Keywords collection you have still taken the time to validate their choice of Keyword. I then talk with the child about the appropriateness of the word and we would determine together if we should include this word in our Keyword collection. As the teacher, you must know what you are comfortable with the children including because you will ultimately have to stand up for the child if the word is ever questioned by an administrator or parent.

7. How do you incorporate Keywords into the school day?

Melissa: Students refer to their Keywords when they write. I also see them flipping through their words at different times of the day and sharing with a friend at their table. If a child asks me how to spell a word and I know another child has that keyword, I may call on him to share the word with his classmate. Other times I use a word a child learned to start off our morning meeting. This happens frequently when kids begin to use content area vocabulary as their Keywords.

Chelsey: My students also refer to their Keywords during writing. They also are aware of each other's words, so they may borrow classmates' words throughout the day.

Joy: In my classroom Keywords is a morning work activity. Students would come in and unpack and then would have the choice of beginning morning work or visiting the Keywords table. Some students would complete morning work first and then visit the table while others would rush straight to Keywords before engaging in any other task. For those students who arrived late, Keywords could be done during a literacy center or anytime during the day that other work was finished. We also would have structured sharing time or word celebrations periodically where students would share with a partner or small group. You could even make this part of your morning carpet time when the students are checking in with you for the day.

8. What do you do if a child never wants to do a Keyword?

Melissa: I have actually never had this happen! If it were to ever happen, I would call on that student periodically and ask if he had thought of a word he would like to learn. I may eventually get the child to come over one day and demonstrate to him what word I would learn and help lead him to identifying a word he would like to learn.

Chelsey: This also has never happened in my classroom. My students are starving for attention, and enjoy the conversation and connectedness that

Keywords provides.

Joy: I always invite students to the Keywords table if I see that they have not chosen a word recently. I will encourage the student to sit and listen to the words of their classmates, listen and join in to the conversations, and then consider if there is a Keyword that they are interested in. I always try to talk with the child about topics of interest to see if this will peak their curiosity of a word that they would like to choose.

9. How long does it take for a child to do a Keyword?

Melissa: From the moment the child sits down to the moment the child gets up with the word stapled on a sentence strip as a crown, I would say it had been five minutes. However, this activity can be easily differentiated depending on the child's needs. Some need more time developing print concepts, while others may need more handwriting instruction.

Chelsey: On average about five minutes for the child, depending on their details. This does not mean it requires five minutes per child of the teacher's attention. The conversation of the Keyword probably lasts about a minute and then I send the child to their desk to complete their writing and drawing while I move on to the next child.

Joy: Some students know their routine and take only about five minutes to complete their Keyword, write about it, and share. Others will take between fifteen and twenty minutes to complete their Keyword. Really it all depends on the child, their routine, and how involved they become with their Keyword.

10. What rationale do you use for taking time daily to do Keywords? Has a principal ever challenged this use of time?

Melissa: Keywords is one of my favorite instructional tools. I actually find myself looking forward to this time with my students. Keywords methodology provides a meaningful context for learning. I am able to teach objectives using material that is both meaningful and familiar to my students. It allows me to get to know my students and build a personal relationship with them; it makes them realize they have a unique voice and story to share and provides a means for them to do so. I like how Keyword is student-centered, gives value to the child, and allows them to take pride in their individuality. I have not yet had an administrator challenge my use of Keywords, but they have questioned it.

Chelsey: For many students, reading is something that is not exciting to them because they struggle with it or they have not encountered the value of reading yet. Keywords methodology has shown time and time again that it is enjoyable and provides the opportunity for that spark of enjoyment of reading to occur. I have not had an administrator question the use of Keywords in my classroom.

Joy: Keywords is one of the most rewarding parts of the day in my classroom for me and the students. It is a time for students to self-select meaningful vocabulary and use these words in a meaningful context. Keywords is student centered and student motivated. It encourages daily sharing and conversations between teacher and student and student to student. The children show ownership for their words and take pride in sharing what they have chosen. It gives me a chance to validate the children's word choices, their feelings, and conversations. Keywords practice increase written and spoken vocabulary and gives everyone in the classroom an opportunity to learn about each other.

I have used Keywords in my classroom under several different administrators. Administrators have always been supportive of Keywords especially those that have taken the time to observe. I have worked in schools that were receiving government funding or grants that wanted protected blocks of time where Keywords was not initially accepted as an appropriate use of time during these protected blocks. With enough passion for Keywords and the willingness to stand up for what you know works for your students even these folks will come around.

## *Chapter 10*
## So What Have We Learned?

Today's literacy climate is often perceived by teachers as restrictive. Learning is perceived as linear, predictable and scripted for one-size-fits-all. Sylvia Ashton-Warner wrote fifty years ago of her struggle to teach effectively in a similar climate—one that did not recognize the unique language and cultures that her children brought into the classroom. Within this divisive climate Ashton-Warner understood that the curriculum she was asked to teach conflicted with what she observed daily with the children. The language they used, their reaction to their names, labels and semantically rich words when seen in print were disconnected with stories from their school texts. She became determined to lead them to connecting "organic language" to print. She was so impressed with her results that she rebelled against the imposed structure and invented a curriculum to validate her children's inner, organic texts.

In my own work using Keywords, or organic language, I have witnessed a disconnect with programmed texts compared to the excitement and success of a child seeing his or her own Keywords in print. "Owning their words" is a descriptive phrase for the child's connection between the spoken and written word. Three current teachers tell their stories here of how they have taken up this process from Ashton-Warner's texts for practice in their own classrooms. Other teachers' stories are also included, showing adaptations created to fit the classroom and children's needs. All participating teachers felt that Keywords complimented and supported the larger guidelines suggested—or in some cases, mandated—by the state. In other words they felt secure in using twenty –thirty minutes a day—or more, as in Joy's case—for Keywords. In one classroom Melissa said of her kindergarteners, "I am so excited at the power these words give to my kindergarteners."

Keywords methodology has helped children learn to love words and to become excited about reading. It is because the words are theirs. They own them. Sight words are not meaningful to children. They are often unable to make connections. As one teacher put it, "Of course we need to teach these words, but they should not be the first words children learn. I feel we need to stop drilling and skilling these words because often times they are not developmentally appropriate…I have been able to use the idea of Keywords and fit it into a better idea for reading instruction."

The ongoing challenge facing the use of Keywords in classrooms today is helping teachers to see the value of Keywords in comparison to a more controlled approach. Does a school promote a direct instruction program for the teaching of vocabulary and phonics or use a teacher derived lists of words? Is the classroom open for child-selected words and a holistic and integrated view of vocabulary development? Next, we have to consider teachers' philosophies and how this impacts the use of Keywords in the classroom. Is the teacher willing to give control to children through allowing choice? Is the teacher willing to authentically converse with children and devote time to developing conversations around their words? Will the teacher find this strategy to be as rewarding as the children do?

The practice speaks for itself. For those of us who have discovered this extraordinary methodology, we are already experiencing the excitement of organic language.

*Appendix A*

Sample Kindergarten Keywords

| Kindergarten Boy | Kindergarten Boy | Kindergarten Boy | Kindergarten Boy |
|---|---|---|---|
| Spiderman | army | Rudolph | Shanika |
| run | April | Jose | Twana |
| cat | go-cart | Steven | lottery ticket |
| mom | bird | Panda bear | marker |
| Logan | American flag | Matthew | |
| | racecar | | |
| | Optimus Prime© | | |
| | Spiderman | | |
| | | | |
| Kindergarten Girl | Kindergarten Girl | Kindergarten Girl | Kindergarten Girl |
| bird | Maria | horse | Ella |
| Gingerbread man | dog | caballo | sister |
| Chica | Lois Ehlert | robot | Eric Carle |
| fish | llama | like | unicorn |
| turtle | cat | Laura Numeroff | bag |
| Miss Milstead | | Eric Carle | Jojo |
| Sherice | | | mom |
| | | | glass |
| | | | slipper |
| | | | Baby |

*Appendix B*

Sample First Grade Keywords

| 1st Grade Boy | 1st Grade Boy | 1st Grade Boy | 1st Grade Boy |
|---|---|---|---|
| Fall | Mrs. Lunsford | Tank | I love you Drew |
| Winter | Matthew | Cop | Savannah |
| Spring | Donald | Donald | Stapler |
| | Ms. Bahlman | Monster truck | |
| | Tree | | |
| | Thomas | | |
| | | | |
| 1st Grade Boy | 1st Grade Boy | 1st Grade Boy | |
| One hundred | Ms. Bahlman | Mississippi | |
| Turtle | Gorilla | Feeling | |
| Glove | Chipmunk | Trick | |
| Scooby Dog | Alvin | Sick | |
| Snowman | | sack | |
| | | | |
| 1st Grade Girl | 1st Grade Girl | 1st Grade Girl | 1st Grade Girl |
| Troy | Troy | Rose | Husky |
| Fish | Pixie | Horse | Wolf |
| Mrs. Lunsford | Taniya | Puppy | Pony |
| Ms. Bahlman | Playground | Armadillo | Scribble |
| pig | Snow | Butterfly | Daisy |
| Spider | Seth | Snow | Cheetah |
| Stickers | | lamb | horse |
| Big | | hamster | |
| Turkey | | fish | |
| Horse | | sheep | |
| Haley | | Bird | |
| | | Easter | |
| | | duck | |

| $1^{st}$ Grade Girl | $1^{st}$ Grade Girl | $1^{st}$ Grade Girl | $1^{st}$ Grade Girl |
|---|---|---|---|
| Book | Jason | Taniya | Gorilla |
| Alexis | Pearls | Chipmunk | Puppy |
| Ms. Bahlman | Florida | Happy Birthday | Haley |
| Angel | Pine tree | | |
| Brittany | Zac Efron | | |

*Appendix C*
Sample Second Grade Keywords

| 2nd Grade Boy | 2nd Grade Boy | 2nd Grade Boy | 2nd Grade Boy |
|---|---|---|---|
| Crane | Basketball | February 1st | Deer |
| Baseball | Trampoline | Happy Feet | Fire |
| X box | Music | Police officer | Nest |
| Simpsons | Video | Post office | Leash |
| Country | Basketball game | Dirt bike | Water |
| Christmas | Thanksgiving | China | Sing |
| Gameboy | New York | Happy New Year | Company |
| Baby brother | Gameboy Advanced | Apartment | Cake |
| Driver's license | Sand board | Tiger | Snowflake |
| Pine Valley | tournament | Football | November |
| cars | | Christmas | Wish |
| | | Computer lab | Chair |
| | | Parade | Basket |
| | | Penguin | Lunchbox |
| | | Award | Hotdog |
| | | Special | Pencil |
| | | County | Ring |
| | | Director | Grass |
| | | Ferris wheel | Truck |
| | | Compound | Window |
| | | Celebration | Keyboard |
| | | Soldier | Chowder |
| | | Coach | Key |
| | | Ipod | Jump |
| | | graduating | Mall |
| | | | Sunflower |
| | | | Cats |
| | | | Fireworks |

| | | | |
|---|---|---|---|
| | | | Train |
| | | | Table |
| | | | Snowdog |
| | | | Eggs |
| | | | pen |
| | | | |
| 2nd Grade Girl | 2nd Grade Girl | 2nd Grade Girl | 2nd Grade Girl |
| Valentines Day | Dictionary | Ms. Foster | Jaden |
| Anniversary | Movies | Mommy dog and baby puppies | Grandma |
| Chris Brown | Hannah Montana | Beyonce | Picture |
| Super | Rainforest | Isaiah | Calculator |
| Soldier girl | Lifeguard | Sparkly | Birthday |
| Graduate | Fog | Markers | Constitution |
| Cicis Pizza | Enchanted | Texas Chainsaw | Festival |
| Gail (?) | Celebration | 3 ninjas | Christmas |
| Difficult | President | Halloween | Music |
| Friends | Space | Peacock | Magnet seat |
| Exclamation mark | London Tiptim | Welcome Inn | Hanukkah |
| Cyber chase | United States | Strawberry | Jahein |
| Excited | Race car | Toothbrush | Jac'Queal |
| Certificate | Section 8 | Katrell | Scarf |
| Jellybean | | Lawanda | Under |
| Rick Ross | | Gloves | Martin Luther King, Jr |
| Dark | | Silver | Sleepover |
| Drama | | Water | Leather |
| Birthday party | | Heelys | Shalaya |
| X box | | Country | Born |
| Bratz | | Gingerbread Man | Disney World |
| May 4 | | | Buried |
| Soldier | | | Family pictures |
| Hanukkah | | | Aaliyah |
| | | | |
| 2nd Grade Girl | | | |
| New shoes | | | |
| Hole puncher | | | |
| Doctor | | | |
| Field trip | | | |
| Snow boots | | | |
| Uniform | | | |

| | | | |
|---|---|---|---|
| Hamster | | | |
| Turkey | | | |
| One hundred | | | |
| Dog | | | |
| Happy Anniversary | | | |
| Hay ride | | | |
| Holiday | | | |
| Love | | | |
| Tim | | | |
| Christmas | | | |
| Multiplication | | | |
| Santa Claus | | | |
| Glasses | | | |
| Flat iron | | | |
| Snowman | | | |
| Alligator | | | |
| Cereal | | | |
| Brother | | | |
| Rose | | | |
| Green bus | | | |
| Gift | | | |
| Crystal | | | |
| Study | | | |
| Mom | | | |
| May 4th | | | |
| Hairdo | | | |
| Mrs. Carol | | | |
| Sleepover | | | |
| Davon | | | |
| Happy New Year | | | |
| Adora | | | |
| Doctor | | | |
| Uncle Gresad | | | |

## Bibliography


Ashton-Warner, Sylvia. *Greenstone (*New Zealand: Whitcombe and Tombs, 1966).

———. *I Passed This Way* (Wellington: Reed, 1980).

———. *Myself (*New Zealand: Whitcombe and Tombs, 1967).

———. *Spearpoint. (*New York: Knopf, 1972).

———. *Spinster. (*London: Secker and Warburg, 1958).

———. *Teacher* (New York: Simon & Schuster, 1963).

*Beverly Hills Chihuahua*, film, directed by Raja Gosnell (2008, Los Angeles: Walt Disney Pictures).

Brabham, Edna and Villaume, Susan "Vocabulary instruction: Concerns and visions," *The Reading Teacher* 56, (2002): 264-268.

Clemens, Sydney G. *Pay Attention to the Children: Lessons for Teachers and Parents from Sylvia Ashton-Warner* (Napa, California: Rattle OK Publications).

Hruby, George. "Sociological, Postmodern, and New Realism Perspectives in Social Constructionism: Implications for Literacy Research," *Reading Research Quarterly* 36, no. 1 (2001): 48-62.

International Reading Association's Summary of National Reading Panel Report: accessed April 10, 2008, http://www.reading.org/resources/issues/reports/nrp.html.

Jaeger, Beth. "Silencing Teachers in an Era of Scripted Reading," *Rethinking Schools* 20, no. 3 (2006): 40.

Lee, Clara. "The mathematics of language acquisition," (2007): accessed April 10, 2008, http://arstenchica.com/journals/science.ars/2007/08/02/the-mathematics-of-language-acquisition.

Lemman, Nicholas. "The Reading Wars," *Atlantic Monthly* 280, no. 5 (1997): 128-134, accessed Dec. 28, 2011, http://talimihaqschool.blogspot.com/Looking_from_here/November 5 2006.

Mamchur, Carolyn. "Heart Beat," *Educational Leadership* 40, no. 4 (1983): 14-20.

Macquillan, Jeff. *The Literary Crisis: False Claims, Real Solutions* (Portsmouth, NH: Heinemann 1998).

Middleton, Susan. "Sylvia's Place: Ashton-Warner as New Zealand Educational Theorist" in The Kiss and the Ghost: Sylvia Ashton-Warner and New Zealand, eds. A. Jones and S. Middleton (Sense Publishers, 2009), 39-49.

National Education Foundation. Maori Infant Room: Organic Reading and the Key Vocabulary (New Zealand: National Education, 1 December 1955): 392–393.

Neuman, Susan and Donna Celano. "Access to Print in Low-Income and Middle-Income Communities: An Ecological Study of Four Neighborhoods," *Reading Research Quarterly*, 36, (2003): 8-26.

Neumeyer, Peter. "The Art of the Word: Significance in Stories for Young People," *The English Journal* 66, no. 5 (1977): 28.

Schacher, Judy. Skippyjon Jones (Los Angeles: Scholastic, 2006).

Thompson, Nancy. "Sylvia Ashton-Warner: Reclaiming Personal Meaning in Literacy Teaching," *The English Journal* 89, no. 3 (2000).

*Two Loves*, film, directed by Charles Walters (1961, Los Angeles: Metro-Goldwyn-Mayer).

Veatch, Jeannette. "From the Vantage of Retirement," *The Reading Teacher* 49, no. 7 (1996): 510-516.

Wasserman, Selma. "Dare to be Different: Can a School Choose its Own Path Despite the Pressures of Accountability?" *Phi Delta Kappa*, 88, no.5 (2007): 384.